CULTURE SHOCK! Japan

Rex Shelley

Graphic Arts Center Publishing Company
Portland, Oregon

In the same series

Argentina
Australia
Austria
Belgium
Bolivia
Borneo
Brazil
Britain
California
Canada
Chile
China
Cuba
Czech Republic
Denmark
Ecuador
Egypt
Finland
France
Germany
Greece
Hong Kong
Hungary
India
Indonesia
Iran
Ireland
Israel
Italy
Japan
Korea
Laos
Malaysia
Mauritius
Mexico
Morocco
Myanmar
Nepal
Netherlands
Norway
Pakistan
Philippines
Scotland
Singapore
South Africa
Spain
Sri Lanka
Sweden
Switzerland
Syria
Taiwan
Thailand
Turkey
UAE
Ukraine
USA
USA—The South
Venezuela
Vietnam

Barcelona At Your Door
Chicago At Your Door
Havana At Your Door
Jakarta At Your Door
Kuala Lumpur, Malaysia At Your Door
London At Your Door
Moscow At Your Door
New York At Your Door
Paris At Your Door
Rome At Your Door
San Francisco At Your Door

A Globe-Trotter's Guide
A Parent's Guide
A Student's Guide
A Traveler's Medical Guide
A Wife's Guide

Living and Working Abroad
Personal Protection At Home & Abroad
Working Holidays Abroad

Illustrations by TRIGG

Third edition 1999
Reprinted 1996, 1997, 1998, 2000, 2001, 2002

This book is published by special
arrangement with Times Media Private Limited
Times Centre, 1 New Industrial Road, Singapore 536196
International Standard Book Number 1-55868-071-3
Library of Congress Catalog Number 92-81941
Graphic Arts Center Publishing Company
P.O. Box 10306 • Portland, Oregon 97296-0306 • (503) 226-2402

Printed in Singapore

CONTENTS

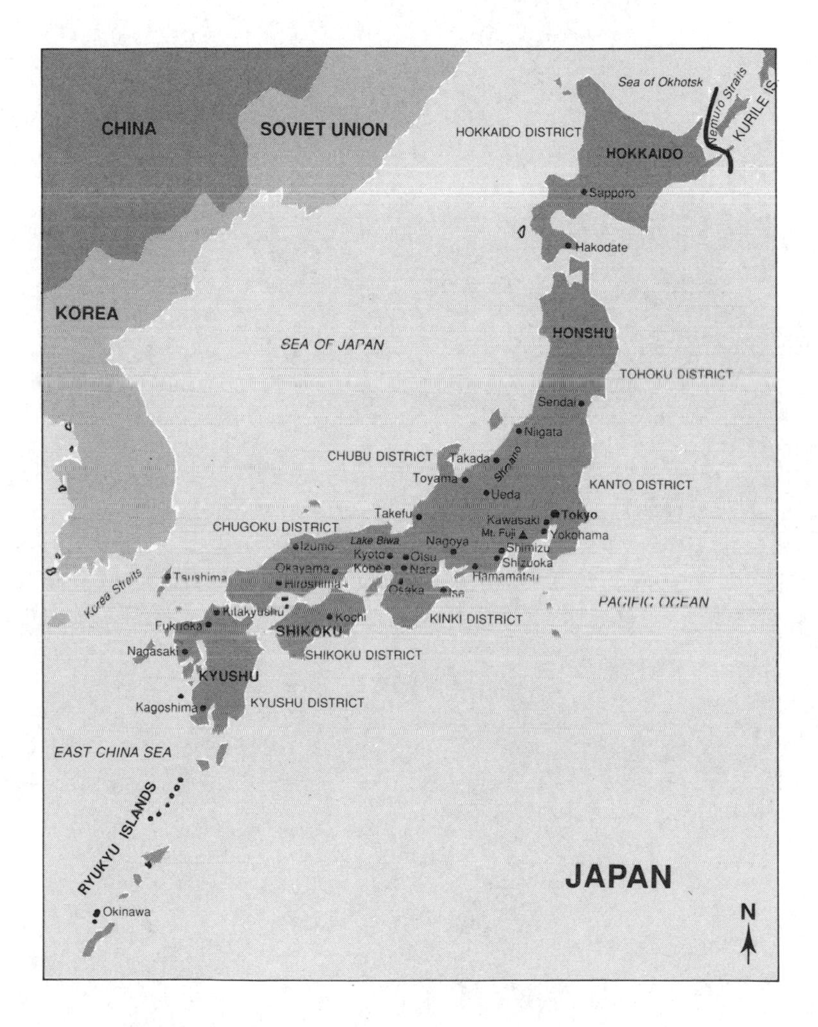
CHINA
SOVIET UNION
Sea of Okhotsk
Nemuro Straits
KURILE IS.
HOKKAIDO DISTRICT
HOKKAIDO
Sapporo
Hakodate
KOREA
SEA OF JAPAN
HONSHU
TOHOKU DISTRICT
Sendai
Niigata
CHUBU DISTRICT
Takada
Shinano
Toyama
Ueda
KANTO DISTRICT
Takefu
Tokyo
Kawasaki
CHUGOKU DISTRICT
Mt. Fuji
Yokohama
Lake Biwa
Nagoya
Izumo
Kyoto
Otsu
Shimizu
Okayama
Kobe
Nara
Shizuoka
Tsushima
Hiroshima
Hamamatsu
Osaka
Ise
Kurea Straits
PACIFIC OCEAN
Kitakyushu
Kochi
KINKI DISTRICT
Fukuoka
SHIKOKU
Nagasaki
SHIKOKU DISTRICT
KYUSHU
Kagoshima
KYUSHU DISTRICT
EAST CHINA SEA
RYUKYU ISLANDS
JAPAN
Okinawa
N

— Chapter One —

INTRODUCTION

This book has one objective: to help you cope with the culture shock of Japan. Culture shock Japan is the total effect of thc surprises a stranger encounters when shc or hc first sets foot in Japan. The things that may startle you and throw you off balance, especially if you have come to Japan to live for a few years, are highlighted and explained, and tips on how to cope with the surprises are given.

If you are only going there as a tourist, knowing what the culture shock of Japan is and how it can be overcome will give you a deeper insight into the Japanese.

It is assumed that you know nothing at all about Japan and the

Japanese. We will start from square one, which is the basic geography, economy and history of the people; a thumbnail profile of Japan.

JAPAN

Japan is a group of islands lying off the eastern coast of the huge Asian continent, between the latitude parallels of 20 and 46 degrees north of the equator. It is the easternmost part of Asia. Japan consists of four main islands and about 6,850 smaller islands. The four main islands are, from north to south, Hokkaido (literally, the north sea way), Honshu (literally, the original, the base island), Shikoku (the four countries), and Kyushu (nine regions).

The total land area is about one and a half times as large as Britain and slightly smaller than the state of California. Japan is a mountainous country; about 70–80% of the land is covered by mountains and volcanoes, many of which are still active. Only about 15% of the land is arable, and less than 10% of the country is residential land.

The highest mountain is Mount Fuji, an inactive volcano of majestic beauty, 3,776 metres high. It is within a day's trip from Tokyo. The Japanese call it Fujisan but *san* here means 'mountain' and not 'mister'. The Japanese have a deep reverence for nature and all things physically beautiful. Mount Fuji has become the symbol of purity and constancy to them. Countless poems have been written around it, and innumerable paintings of Fujisan have been made over the centuries.

There are about 60 active volcanoes in Japan, and the country gets an average of 1,500 volcanic tremors a year. The Japanese take these as a matter of course. They enjoy the beauty of their volcanoes and the hot springs around them. One of the well known volcanoes is Mihara. It is a favourite spot for lovers' double suicides.

The most famous lake in the country is Lake Biwa near the city of Kyoto. The Inland Sea, enclosed between the islands of Honshu,

Excellent opportunities exist in Japan for mountain climbing in summer.

Japan's serene inland sea.

Shikoku and Kyushu, is one of the most picturesque places in Japan.

Japan is divided into 47 regional divisions consisting of

- one *dou* (Hokkaido)
- one *toh* (Tokyo-toh – Metropolis)
- two *fu* (Osaka-fu and Kyoto-fu)
- 43 *ken* (prefectures)

The capital, Tokyo, is situated on the eastern coast somewhere in the middle of Honshu.

Japan has a temperate climate. Spring and fall are crisp and pleasant, with temperatures averaging 15°C (59°F). Summer is hot and humid and the temperature can go up to as high as 36°C (97°F). Humidity can reach 84%. Winter is usually dry with many days of bright blue skies. In Tokyo winter lows can run down to 5°C (41°F). Hokkaido and some northern and eastern parts of Honshu have bitter winters with heavy snowfalls.

There is a rainy season in June and another in early July, and typhoons blow in from the South China Sea between August and October.

These are generalisations for Japan. With the islands stretching about 2,800 km from north to south, roughly between the same latitudes of Maine and Georgia, or Morocco and Paris, there is considerable variation in climate over the country. Weather changes can be rapid and abrupt. Weather forecasting is difficult under these conditions.

Population Distribution

All told, with its mountains, volcanoes, earthquakes and typhoons, it is a harsh land that has bred a rugged, inward-looking people.

Japan's population was estimated to be 126 million in 1998. About 70% of the population lives along the coastal plain between Tokyo and the northern part of Kyushu, which includes the major cities of Yokohama, Osaka, Nagoya and Kobe. Tokyo alone has about 12 million inhabitants, making it one of the most populous cities in the world.

Since there is very little flat land in Japan suitable for residential use, population densities are very high: 332 people per square kilometre in Japan, and 11,544 people per square kilometre in Tokyo. Population growth has slowed down in recent years, averaging 0.91% between 1985 and 1990.

There are a few groups of ethnic minorities in Japan: Ainu, the aboriginal people of the country, Koreans and Okinawans.

Foreign residents numbered about 1,075,500 in 1990. The largest groups are Koreans, Chinese and Americans. Among them there were about 38,450 foreign students, mostly from the Republic of China (Taiwan), Korea, the People's Republic of China, Hong Kong and other Asian countries.

GOVERNMENT AND ROYALTY

Japan was the first Asian country to establish a parliamentary system although the vote was not given to the people at once. The Imperial Diet, their parliament, was set up in 1890. It was part of what historians call the Meiji Restoration, a deliberate plan to change Japan from a feudal kingdom to a modern state. While thousands of Japanese studied all things new in the technical and artistic fields, small teams examined the legalities and administrative systems of leading countries in the world during the Meiji Restoration. They had the opportunity to select and piece together a system that suited them, unfettered by colonial ties or prejudices. They created their Diet, but kept the sovereignty in the hands of the Emperor. A full democratic system was only set up after World War II, in 1946.

The Diet comprises upper and lower houses, members of which are elected by universal suffrage. It is the national legislative body that has the power to carry out all the administrative functions of a government. The prime minister is elected by the Diet.

The main political parties in Japan are:

Liberal Democratic Party
Social Democratic Party
Sakigake (Harbinger)
Democratic Party of Japan
Japan Communist Party
Komei
Liberal Party
New Peace Party
Reform Club

The Imperial family of Japan is said to be descended from an unbroken lineage of nearly two thousand years. No other royal family in the history of mankind has ever been able to hold its position for so long. The present Emperor, Akihito, is the 125th to sit on the Imperial Chrysanthemum throne. The origins of the family are obscure and clouded with records that mix reality with strange and curious myths, but historians generally agree that the first Emperor emerged about the time of the birth of Christ.

The Imperial family has survived through the centuries because it never became fully embroiled in political conflicts. Successive

His Majesty, Emperor Akihito, in the traditional robe, the sokutai, *at the Enthronement Ceremony in November 1990.*

Her Majesty, Empress Michiko, in the traditional twelve-layered robe, the juni-hitoe, *at the Enthronement Ceremony in November 1990.*

military rulers generally left the Imperial family alone, keeping the Imperial court and its retainers unmolested and uncontaminated by vengeance, greed and desire to take total power. They kept the Emperor as the symbolic head of state. This reflects the Japanese approach of seeking compromise rather than rushing into confrontation and flaunting superiority to resolve conflicts.

The Japanese use the reigns of their Emperors as reference points for dates. Thus in the last reign, known as Showa, the years are counted from the date when the Emperor Hirohito ascended the throne. 1985 was the 60th year of Showa, and 1988 the 63rd year, or Showa 63. The present reign is Heisei, which roughly translates as 'Peace and Concord'. 1992 is the fourth year of Heisei.

The Japanese have a deep respect for their Emperor although today he has no real power. When Emperor Hirohito died in 1989 these feelings surfaced, dispelling speculations that the old reverence for the Imperial family had been eroded over the years. The following account by William E. Smith in *Time*, 16 January 1989, describes the scene as the Emperor Hirohito lay dying in the Imperial Palace.

"By the hundreds of thousands, they kept a vigil outside the palace gates through the autumn and early winter. As his struggle went into a third month and then a fourth, they followed every scrap of news on his waning condition; the life of the nation contracted and became more somber in a display of 'self restraint' and respect. When finally they learned that he had died … 122 million citizens were profoundly moved. Some wept, some prayed …"

A BRIEF HISTORY

The history of the Japanese starts at about the time of Christ. Scholars differ in their opinions on events before Christ as there is limited data available. Two chronicles – the *Kojiki* and the *Nihon Shoki* – written in the 8th century AD, which describe an elaborate mythology, are the major sources of information.

The Japanese are a Mongoloid race. Migrants from China, Korea and Manchuria came across the Tsushima strait to southwestern Honshu and to Kyushu. Some scholars have suggested that migrants may also have been people of Malay stock from Oceania.

When they arrived in Japan they found an aboriginal people who were strange and uncivilised to them. These were the Ainu, a Neolithic people more Caucasian than Mongoloid, with hairy skin and round eyes. The Ainu had no written language. They had an animist religion in which the bear had an important role. They fought the intruders fiercely and it was several centuries before the Japanese succeeded in subduing them. There are still Ainu in Japan today, in Hokkaido, where they had retreated to over the centuries.

Some of their beliefs and language still remain in Japanese culture. The name Fujiyama (Mount Fuji), has an Ainu language origin. Akkeshi, in Hokkaido, which is reputed to have the best oysters in Japan, means 'where the oysters are' in the Ainu language. Many of the Shinto religious rites are derived from Ainu rites and beliefs.

The migrants from the Asian continent slowly penetrated the whole country. They had their feuds and their struggles for territory. Eventually one strong man emerged – Jimmu Tenno, the first of the line of the Imperial family.

Heian: In the Heian period (about AD 794 to 1185) there was relative peace, and the arts flourished. This was the time of the great Japanese literary work, *The Tale of the Genji*, written by Lady Murasaki in 1002–19. It was the golden age of Japanese classical literature. Hence the Heian period: the period of peace and calm.

Kamakura: In 1185 Minamoto Yoritomo (throughout this book we use the Japanese style of names, surname first) took control of the country and established his military seat of government at Kamakura, away from the Imperial court at Kyoto. Power passed from the court aristocracy to the military supremo, the *shogun*. It was in this period of the Kamakura *shogunate* that the warrior ethical code of the *samurai* was developed. Religion and the arts went through a phase of simplification, secularisation and popularisation.

Ashikaga: After the fall of the Kamakura *shogunate* in 1333, the Ashikaga family took over. Their regime lasted until 1573 or 1574.

Warring period: Japan was then a feudal society. The mountainous terrain made central control difficult and the country was split into changing alignments of warring states. Regional sufficiency became important and there was considerable development of industries, transportation and public works.

One curious effect of this opening up of opportunity to individuals was that some *samurai* went into seafaring ventures, combining commerce with piracy. They raided the coastal regions of China and contributed in a way to the downfall of the Ming Dynasty.

The 16th century was a century of major events in the history of Japan. The period saw the rise of three of the greatest men in Japanese history: Oda Nobunaga, Toyotomi Hideyoshi and Tokugawa Ieyasu. These were the men who unified the country and set the stage for the dawning of modern Japan.

Oda Nobunaga subjugated his rivals by exploiting the crude muskets that were being made in central Japan, copying what the Portuguese had brought in. In 1578 he was the leading figure in the land and he set himself the task of bringing the whole of Japan under the control of a single powerful authority. He was assassinated in 1582. Toyotomi Hideyoshi and Tokugawa Ieyasu continued the work he began.

Toyotomi Hideyoshi stands out as a powerful and dynamic character in this succession. A small ugly man, almost a dwarf, a man with physical strength and charm, he took over from Oda Nobunaga, setting up several institutions and systems to develop the country. He once told some Jesuits that he would subdue the Chinese empire and force the Chinese to adopt Christianity. Later he moved strongly against the Christians when he saw that Christianity brought more problems than good to the country. Japan enjoyed a certain prosperity and stability under him.

Tokugawa Ieyasu, who followed Toyotomi Hideyoshi, established his position at the battle of Sekigahara against his rivals in 1600. In 1603 he secured for himself the title of *shogun*. He was a cool, unshakeable man of iron. He had spent 40 years fighting and had not only developed into a military commander of the highest calibre, but was also reputed to be a faultless judge of men. Among the instructions which he is believed to have left to his successors is this: "The strong manly ones in life are those who understand the meaning of the word *patience*."

In the middle of the 16th century the first ships from the west began to arrive in Japan. They came bristling with Christian missionaries, who made amazing progress with their conversions. But they also brought the smooth bore musket that changed the strategies of feudal battles and the designs of Japanese castles.

With this flow of Portuguese and Dutch into southern Japan came a most unusual Englishman, Will Adams. He worked his way up through the corridors of power and became a trusted adviser of Tokugawa Ieyasu. Later he betrayed the trust placed in him by working with the Portuguese and Spanish against the Japanese.

It is the story of Will Adams – an almost incredible one – that lies behind Clavell's *Shogun*. Will Adams was the forerunner of several outstanding westerners who came to an insular country suspicious of foreigners, won their respect and trust and influenced their directions of change. One was Fenollosa, who played a major role in the revival of *kabuki* theatre. When he died on a trip to England, the Japanese government sent a warship to bring his body back 'home'. Another is the American, Dr W. Edwards Deming, who, after the Pacific War, brought to Japan the philosophy of quality in industrial production. It is a curious series of quirks in the history of man.

But the first westerners, the Christians, brought with them many problems, not the least of which was the rivalry between the Portuguese Jesuits and the Spanish Dominicans. They also stirred up feelings of new loyalties among the Japanese converts and all the conflicts of individuals with the feudal system finally erupted in a terrible siege and battle at Shimabara in Kyushu.

Unification: The Tokugawa *shogun* threw out all foreigners and closed the country to the world in 1637, to consolidate the Tokugawa government's position without any foreign interference. It was a bold, landmark decision. No Japanese was allowed to travel out of Japan, and there was a restriction on the size of boats to ensure this edict's effectiveness. For the next two hundred years Japan was isolated from the world.

They made one exception. They allowed one Dutch ship into Nagasaki every year. This is an example of Japanese practical compromise without affecting the fundamental philosophy. They wanted no part of the mysterious, changing western world, yet there was a practical need for those in power to know what was going on outside.

But the Europeans and the new Americans who were building their colonial empires and exploiting the produce of Asia could not leave Japan alone. In Russia, groups of financiers and traders with their eye on the profits Japan could yield succeeded in persuading their reluctant government to send a fleet all the way round the Cape of Good Hope to Japan. Admiral Putyatin arrived in Nagasaki in August 1853, hoping to force open the closed doors.

He was pipped by an American, Commodore Perry, who had sailed into Edo Bay (now Tokyo) in July with four vessels, two of them powered by steam, and demanded that Japan open its doors to the world. The Americans needed bases for their China trade. In particular, they needed coal for their steamships.

The rulers were startled and shaken by the American intrusion and demands. But they knew, via the trickle of reports about many strange and newfangled things coming in through the Dutch, that they could not defend themselves against the western nations with their new war technology.

They took the painful, bitter, realistic decision and opened the door a little, knowing that this would be only the beginning.

New learning: The country then swung into a period of learning and selective assimilation of all things western with a determination that is unparalleled in human history. Within about 50 years Japan moved through hundreds of years of human thought and development, from a feudal anachronism to a modern nation.

One strange feature of this transformation is that they examined the new concepts and technologies not through the usual process of human contact but by the flow of books and objects. It is perhaps because of this that they came through the period with the inner soul of Japan untainted. And it is because of this unique merging of the West and Asia that *gaijin* (foreigners) find the Japanese today so much like themselves in many ways, yet so different at their core.

There was one notable exception to the generalisation that the Japanese learnt from the West through objects and books. The government in fact employed foreigners to help them move into the 19th century. They called these people *oyatoi-gaijin*. In 1874 their number rose to a peak of 527. There were only 79 in 1895.

Meiji Restoration: In 1866 the Emperor Komei died, and his 15-year-old son took over as the Emperor Meiji in 1867. He was to rule over Japan for 45 years, Japan's great golden era of growth and modernisation. In 1868 the great house of Tokugawa, which had provided Japan with 15 *shogun*, collapsed, and the power went to the Imperial throne.

The Imperial family did not cling on to their newfound power. In the spirit of the changing times they set up a Constitution in 1889 and the Imperial Diet in 1890, the first steps that allowed Japan to mature into a full democracy in 1946.

In the 87 years between 1854, when America forced Japan to open its doors to the world, and the start of the Pacific War, Japan built up a fighting force that first proved its mettle in two short wars.

In 1894 Japan fought against China, first in Korea and later on Chinese soil. To the world's surprise it brought the Asian giant, fossilised in the glory of its past, to its knees. Japan exacted heavy recompensation from China, but Russia, France and Germany intervened, to the bitter resentment of the Japanese, and forced Japan to forgo much of what it had won. The Emperor Meiji met the massive popular indignation with a plea that they should try 'to bear the unbearable'. In 1945 Emperor Hirohito used the same words, knowing his people would understand the poignancy of them, when he told his people Japan had surrendered to the Allied Forces.

A lesser battle in some ways against the Russian fleet during the Russo-Japan war in 1904 had a greater historical impact. This was the battle which western historians know as the Battle of Tsushima and the Japanese call the Battle of the Sea of Japan, *Nihonkai kaisen*. In two days they destroyed the Russian Baltic fleet of 38 vessels that had sailed all the way from Europe. It was the first ever major victory of an Asian nation against the West. It destroyed a myth of European invulnerability, and had far-reaching effects on morale throughout Asia, especially on the nationalists in the colonised territories.

Charged with confidence from the *Nihonkai kaisen*, the militarist elements in the country strengthened, and from then on the history of Japan is a succession of struggles between aggressive factions and moderates. There was much fighting overseas, in China, Korea and Manchuria. In 1895 Japan had taken Formosa (Taiwan) as part of its war prizes from China. In 1910 Japan annexed Korea, and ruled it for 35 years. Japan became a player in the international game of military power politics. And it played its cards in the western style of the times, matching their arrogant and expansionist policies.

Pacific War: At home the process of absorbing the best from the modern world continued, though with some problems as the people began to make their protests felt and extremists periodically rose and fell. But all through these years Japan built up its economic muscle, and the militarist factions got their way more often than not, this culminating in the attack on Pearl Harbor on 7 December 1941 that altered the course of not only Japan's history, but also the world's.

The Pearl Harbor attack built a faith and confidence in the Japanese that helped to carry them through the Pacific War. The code words for the attack order, *tora, tora, tora* (tiger, tiger, tiger), were evocative and stirred feelings in the Japanese during the war, as Churchill's 'blood, sweat, toil and tears' did in the English. The Pearl Harbor attack rocked the world. But it was not the first time Japan had struck before it had declared war. It had done it twice before. And when the Japanese navy hit the Russian Baltic fleet before war was declared the British press described it as a 'daring and innovative move'!

Since World War II: The rest is recent history: the seven-year occupation of Japan, the economic boom, the technical and marketing miracles, trade and currency imbalances …

You probably know it all. But most of us have not paused to dwell on the thought that for the second time in history America had intruded into Japan, and for the second time in a hundred years Japan has undergone a transformation beyond what the most optimistic imaginations could have predicted at that time, and become a more stable and far more powerful nation, while keeping its soul still essentially Japanese.

The history of Japan is fascinating. Like all history, it reveals human force, endeavour and weaknesses. And like the history of all peoples, it points to how they have come to be what they are today, and how they think, feel and behave in this 20th century. It is the people, not the physical impact, that gives the tourist and the expatriate who has come to live in a foreign land the real culture shock.

— *Chapter Two* —

THE JAPANESE

Living in another country brings you into direct contact with a new culture and its people. This is what makes staying abroad both exciting and frustrating. If you come to Japan from America or Europe, you will most probably have more knowledge of Japanese products than of the Japanese. You will discover that learning about the culture and lifestyles of the Japanese makes the new world around you more interesting and reduces some of your frustrations.

It is difficult to describe the national characteristics of any people fully in a single chapter. Sketched out in this chapter is a picture of the average Japanese and the more common deviations from the average.

Some more about their customs and social attitudes is described in Chapter 5, which covers the topic of socialising with the Japanese.

Homo economicus, Economic Man

The Japanese work very hard, in spite of having the highest GNP per capita in the world. Their industriousness may surprise you and you may wonder why they keep so hard at it. Most analysts think it is fundamentally because they still believe that their country is poor.

It is a legacy from the war, when Japan, without any significant natural resources, could only survive through the industry of its people and its trade. The need to work hard was felt by every Japanese and sacrificing one's self for the nation became an essential social image to achieve and maintain. It still exists today. Workers don't watch the clock to stop at five. They go on pushing themselves. One can almost say that they just can't stop; that's the way they are today.

But there is another reason: personal financial pressures. The forces of ostentatious consumerism are as strong in Japanese society as they are all over the world. Housing costs keep skyrocketing. So do costs of education and many other ordinary living costs. Advertising has created the feeling of needs for new goods to enjoy life. The pressure to meet rising costs and striving to improve his lifestyle keeps driving the Japanese working man.

The Japanese use the word *sarariman* for male white-collar workers. It comes from the English salaryman. You will keep encountering words like this that they have adopted and pronounce in their manner. Salarymen form a large part of the labour force that has brought about Japan's economic success, and all the international criticism about the consequential massive trade surplus.

In 1985 the average salaryman worked 43.6 hours a week. Although many Japanese companies have adopted a two-day weekend, a Labour Ministry survey showed that in 1986 only 28% of Japanese workers enjoyed a five-day work week, while 78% had a two-day weekend at least once a month. It was also reported that

Japanese workers on the average took only half of their paid annual vacation, which is usually 15 days a year. The government instituted a 5-day work week for all civil servants from spring 1992.

But statistics of the workaholic Japanese must be compared with the total allocation of time in other parts of the world to get the full picture.

A 1991 study, *The Allocation of Time, Empirical Findings, Behavioural Models, and Problems of Measurement*, published by the Swedish Industrial Institute for Economic and Social Research, reported that men work 56 hours a week in Japan, but only 4 hours at home. The American male does 44 hours on the job and 14 at home. The corresponding figures for the Swedes are 40 and 18.

The Japanese have 40 leisure hours a week; Americans, 42; and Swedes, 39. The Japanese spend 8 hours of their leisure time on social activities and 26 hours on passive pastimes such as watching television; Americans, 15 and 21; and Swedes, 10 and 21. The Japanese spend a lot of time in front of the TV set, probably watching baseball and sumo wrestling.

The salaryman leads a hard life. Because housing is so expensive in the cities, he usually lives far out in the suburbs and it takes him about an hour by train and one or two buses to get to the office.

The day may start with a *chorei*, a morning meeting to boost morale and exhort staff to do their very best. Some companies include the company song and light exercises. The *chorei* may be a daily or weekly affair.

From the *chorei* he goes to his desk, which is in a large open office. (Only the head of the department has his own room.) He has been made to believe that his company does that because the open-plan office is better for communications within the department. If he is a salesman he may make a call or two in the morning. Or he may sit in at a meeting with a potential customer in one of the many small meeting rooms. He will take copious notes, recording every detail discussed.

Lunch may be at the company canteen or at a nearby restaurant. He will choose what he fancies from set menus called *teishoku* or *setto*, from the English phrase, set-lunch. It will be a simple meal with his colleagues.

He will be at his desk when the clock strikes five, especially if his boss is still working. Only when he is satisfied that he has given his best to his immediate team and to his company, will he leave. But not directly for home.

The Japanese salaryman relaxes in almost prescribed ways after the day is done. He will either go to a bar with his workmates, where he may really enjoy himself singing, or he will play mahjong, the Chinese game played with ivory blocks. These social activities are an important element of the system. They bring men who work together closer and provide a release from the tensions of the office.

He rarely comes home before midnight.

If he is in the sales department he may spend the evening entertaining customers to drinks and dinner – probably followed by more drinks. He will eat well and drink without fear of showing how tipsy he is, but he will very seldom get too familiar with his customer.

Businessmen stop at their favourite bar after office hours to relax over drinks with their colleagues.

He catches up on lost sleep on the weekends. If he is senior enough he may play golf. Or he may just go out to a driving range and hit balls to improve his drive for the day when he will be able to play a full game on a real course – doggedly preparing himself for the dream. He will spend a fair amount of time over the weekend watching television. Once in a while he will take his family out.

He hands his pay-packet to his wife and leaves her to do all the housework and run the household. He may talk with her before he falls asleep, over breakfast, and on the two or three evenings he is home for dinner. Twice a year, in summer and winter, he gets a bonus. It will be a considerable sum to him, two or three months' salary. This he does not surrender to his wife. They may talk about it and decide to spend it to reduce their mortgage or to save it for their children's education. The priorities of the older salaryman (generally, those born before the war) are quite clear. His company is first; his home, second. *Kigyo-senshi* is another name given to the salaryman – corporate warriors. The battle must be fought and personal needs must stay in the background.

The conflict of a salaryman's dual loyalties to company and family comes into focus when the company decides to send him to another part of Japan or to another country without his family. They call this *tanshin-funin*. He almost invariably accepts the reasoning that as it implies a step up in the organisation, it will be better for his children's education and will not force him to give up the house in which he has invested so much. The result is often alcoholism on the part of the man and a terrible loneliness for his wife.

But not always.

Some Japanese wives heave a great sigh of relief when their husbands bring home the news of a *tanshin-funin*. Her husband is to some extent a burden to her running of the house. He will not do any housework when he is at home. He expects his wife to take care of him and attend to all his needs and wants. Even his children must not be too demanding.

The Japanese husband has a deep-seated psychological block towards housework. He just can't bring himself to work beside his wife, no matter how much he loves her. Her place in the domestic hierarchy was set thousands of years ago, and as far as he is concerned it just cannot change. It is as permanent as the stars in the sky and the mountains of his land.

The women, however, are changing, and so must their men! They call the husband who lounges around watching TV while they slave away the 'cockroach husband'; nothing but a wretched nuisance. A few years ago a TV commercial hit the top in popularity among housewives because it featured the buzz-line 'Husbands should be good, but absent'.

The *kigyo-senshi* committed company warrior is brewing serious problems for himself as Japanese society ages. He has never had time to develop strong interests or hobbies. His life has been dedicated to serving his company and to standard forms of using his limited leisure time, and when he retires, he is lost; a man without a purpose in life. His wife has became a stranger who manages the house, and he finds himself spending the whole day with the woman.

On her part, she has come to regard him as the absent breadwinner over the years and when he stops this basic function he becomes a permanent nuisance. She has to establish a new relationship with this man, a new image and stance towards her retired husband.

Housewives

Behind Japan's economic miracle stand the women who have supported and helped their husbands to rebuild the country into what it is today. "We call our homes and wives 'flat-tops'," says Takemura Kenichi, a prominent social critic, comparing the Japanese woman's role to that of aircraft carriers in the nation's battle for economic supremacy. "Men are the fighter planes. We need the flat-tops to take a rest. But flat-tops never accompany fighter planes to the front."

Traditionally the woman's ideal is to be a perfect *ryosai-kenbo*, a good wife and wise mother. The prime virtue is to sacrifice herself for the family. She has to manage the household finances, run the house, raise her children and provide all the backing and help she can to her husband so that he can devote himself totally to his job. She is driven as hard as her husband drives himself. In her way, she has played her part in the economic growth of Japan.

She spends her day like housewives the world over: shopping, cooking, cleaning, and looking after her children. She gets no help from her man when he is home. She doesn't expect any. But the Japanese housewife, unlike her husband, finds time to indulge in various hobbies such as aerobics or exercise groups – or 'culture classes' to improve herself.

She also carries the burden of pushing her children to study, ensuring that they will have a good start in life when they grow up. This exhortation and pressuring of children to do their utmost in their schoolwork is the norm. The phrase *kyoiku-mama*, education-mama,

The scarf tied from her neck acts as a screen when this Japanese mother nurses her baby.

was coined to describe it.

The great stress on pushing their children is due partly to the housewife finding a purpose and satisfaction in giving her children a good future, and partly to the social and employment systems which in general place a person for life at a level determined by his or her education. Many a bride has learnt soon after marriage the harsh fact that her husband is seldom home. She eventually finds solace from her loneliness in pouring her energy into her children's education.

While the majority of Japanese women are happy to settle down to running their homes, there are many who resent their role very strongly. Middle-aged women in particular, who can look back on their lives of self-sacrifice, slowly build up such resentment. Their feelings are often deep, unexpressed and pent up. Divorce has a bad social stigma. It requires much courage for a Japanese woman to take this step. There are also the financial problems of separation. The common result of such tensions is what the Japanese term *kateinai rikon*, divorced within the home, or living together in the same house but as two separate people.

Divorce also presents a serious problem to men. Having been waited on like lords at home, and quite ignorant of the business of buying food, settling bills and paying for the basics of living, they face practical and often critical psychological problems after a divorce.

The large majority of Japanese women, however, are still content with the compensating security and subtle power of the traditional marriage. They still aspire to be the ideal *ryosai-kenbo*.

Working Women

In 1997, about 40% of Japan's work force were women; approximately 28 million. There are more working women in Japan than unemployed housewives. In the past ten years the female work force has grown by an annual average of 1.3%.

As standards of living improve and ideas from the West trickle in, more and more women, especially younger women, are opting for a working career lifestyle, breaking from the traditions of the past. The career woman is no longer a rarity. Women were first admitted into offices as clerks and servers of tea, but today the opportunities are wide and attractive, in sales and technical jobs, in design, supervisory and administrative positions, and on the factory floors.

But the career women face the same male chauvinism as their counterparts do all over the world. Only 1% of the female work force hold managerial posts compared to 7% of the male. The majority of

Japanese men do not accept women as equals in the working situation. They plug the line of division of labour: men should be in the factories and offices and women in the homes. The more serious argument that working wives would shake the basic social system that allowed men to devote themselves completely to their jobs is also often put forward. A newspaper survey a few years ago showed that 70% of the men who answered would not accept a woman boss. Much of the male resentment against working women is directed at working wives.

The proportion of married women in the female work force rose from 33% in 1962 to 59% in 1989. The married woman worker leads a difficult life. She must run the home when she gets back with no help from her 'cockroach husband'. A government survey in 1986 revealed that the average working woman spends 3 hours and 28 minutes a day on housework and childcare while her average husband spends only 11 minutes. She spends her weekends catching up on her housework back-log.

The career woman has her freedom and spends her leisure time on exercise and sports; swimming and tennis are the most popular. Many career women pursue their chosen lines with the same dedication and zeal as the salarymen. They have to catch up with their housework on weekends and the Japanese career women raise the universal cry that they need 'house-husbands'!

Japanese governments have tried to improve the lot of the working woman, with patchy success. Japan is probably the only country in the world which has a law giving women factory workers leave for their monthly period. However, only a fraction of the women take it. Differential treatment of women workers is prevalent.

In 1985 an Equal Employment Opportunity Law was passed. It covered all aspects of employment from hiring and training to promotion. But it was a piece of legislation without any teeth. Employers have to 'make efforts' to treat women as they treat men and there are no penalties for non-compliance.

Demure and on their best behaviour, to a festival by train.

Children

Children are given a great deal of attention in Japanese families. The Japanese have never adopted the Victorian 'children are seen and not heard' attitude. Japanese children are pampered at home and in public. This pampering is an important part of the upbringing because it makes them dependent on their parents and in the long run teaches them the importance of interdependence with other members of society based on mutual trust. They call this interdependence *amae*.

The Japanese approach to bringing up children is thus diametrically opposed to that of the West, where independence is not only encouraged, but is the goal. When a Japanese couple has a child, the parent-child relationship, or rather the mother-child relationship,

An afternoon devoted to a music class.

becomes much stronger than that between husband and wife. Japanese mothers push their children to achieve high academic performance and smother them with attention. Most Japanese children feel that their mothers are stricter than their fathers.

Japanese children start school at the age of six and are required to complete nine years of compulsory education – six in elementary school and three in junior high school. Many elementary schoolchildren go to *juku*, group tutorial classes, after school or take lessons in aesthetic subjects such as piano playing, ballet or calligraphy. According to a spring 1990 survey of the Nagoya-based Tokai Bank, parents pay as much as US$3,600–4,800 per year for these lessons.

At school they are taught various subjects rigorously and are trained to socialise with others in a harmonious manner. 'Being considerate to others' and 'Not causing discomfort to others' are two maxims often emphasised in school. Ruth Benedict, in *The Chrysanthemum and the Sword*, says:

"'You must respect yourself' is constantly on parents' lips in admonishing their adolescent children, and it refers to observing proprieties and living up to other people's expectation. ... When a parent says to them, 'You did not behave as a self-respecting person should,' it means that they are accused of an impropriety rather than lack of courage to stand up for a right.

Since a few years ago there has been a lot of criticism of schools which over-discipline and over-regiment their students. Some social critics have said that these strict school regulations, added to pressures to study hard, have made children take out their frustrations on less assertive children at school by bullying. This bullying, called *ijime*, has become so prevalent that the government has set up a task force to deal with the problem.

The activities of Japanese children after school consist of *juku* and other lessons, watching TV, reading comics and playing with their friends. Most of them have their own desks and bicycles and many have a watch and a radio cassette recorder. Computer games, pianos and other musical instruments are also popular possessions. The average Japanese child helps with the household chores for only about ten minutes a day. They are less interested in sports and volunteer activities than children in the United States and West Germany.

Teenagers

Studying hard for university entrance examinations preoccupies many teenagers. As in their earlier years, they attend the *juku* because entering the right university is of the utmost importance to a Japanese. It determines what prestigious companies she or he will be employed by and thus the future stability of their lives. These examinations are fiercely competitive. The entrance examinations force them to drop all other activities and spend their time studying.

Teenagers' blossoming interest in the opposite sex is sternly discouraged by parents and schools, and often stoically suppressed by them themselves, so that they will not be unnecessarily distracted from their studies. The Japanese teenager's life is not half as exciting as that of the western teenager. In rare moments when they have some free time they may spend it with their friends at their homes, or at a coffee shop or at the movies. There is no real partying until they get into a university.

Although almost all students move up to high school, only about 30–36% of high school graduates go on to junior colleges or universities. And of these, only a small number make it to the top universities, public or private. Many high school students aspire to get into the very best universities, such as Tokyo University, known as Todai. Those who fail their entrance examinations take an extra year or sometimes a few years after they leave high school to attend special preparatory schools so that they will pass the examinations the next time. This is quite common. Students in these 'prep' schools are called *ronin*, wandering warriors, to distinguish them from other students. They will often visit shrines or temples to buy good luck charms for success in the examinations.

But once they get into a university the pressure falls off. They do not have to study as hard as they did for the entrance examinations. The four years at the university are considered by many to be a leisurely break between the fiercely competitive studying of their pre-university days and the harsh workaholic life ahead of them. It is indeed the most relaxed time they will ever have. Life on campus is good for the Japanese student. Companies recruiting graduates rate university club activities and part-time work highly, believing that students have learnt social skills and teamwork cooperation through these extracurricular pursuits.

Not all students go into the university feeling free and relaxed after their hard spell of studying for the entrance examinations. Some feel a serious let-down soon after they start the first year in April. University final examinations are in late February or early March. There is a similar feeling of depression when the pressure of examinations has passed.

Suicides are not uncommon in May as reactions rise to a peak after a delay. They call this *gogatsu-byo*, sometimes translated into English as the 'May Syndrome'.

Suicide

The Japanese word for suicide is *jisatsu*. Yes, it's *jisatsu*, not *harakiri*. Nor is it *kamikaze*.

Harakiri or belly-cutting is the commonly used word for the ritualistic suicide formally known as *seppuku*. It is a formal ceremony with a whole set of rules dealing with the location, the size of the area, details of how the stomach should be cut, and who can commit *harakiri*. An important part of the ritual is the helper, *kaishaku*, usually a very close friend. He chops off the head of the man committing *harakiri* as a final part of the act.

It was part of the *samurai* code. It was either a demonstration of honour, courage, moral character, a show of contempt to the enemy, a protest against injustice, a self-sacrifice to save others – or it was ordered as a punishment by the feudal lord or *shogun*.

It is interesting to note that *harakiri* was only adopted after Buddhism came to Japan, bringing with it its philosophy of the transitory nature of life and the glory of death. There have been several attempts in the past to stop the practice, but

none were successful. It fits in with the Japanese psyche of feeling intense shame when one has done something ghastly.

Kamikaze, the divine wind, was the phrase the Japanese coined for the storm that destroyed an invasion fleet many hundred years ago. It was taken up during the war to describe the suicide pilots.

The frequency of suicide in Japan does not differ from that in other countries, although the frequency of lovers' suicides is probably higher. Suicide, however, does not have the sinful implications it does in Christianity.

Adulthood

There is a traditional rite of passage into adulthood in Japan, which is performed on 15 January every year. It is called *Seijin-no-hi*, literally the Day of Adults. Although it is a social rite, it is sponsored by local government authorities and held in public places. The young adults wear their best *kimono* or western outfits (especially the males) and have their photographs taken at studios. Adulthood is reached at 20 in Japan. The law prohibits anyone below 20 from drinking or smoking, although in practice it is not enforced.

Sex

It is very difficult to make generalisations about attitudes towards sex in Japan. It is true that the old books record many accounts of rather free sexual relations in the farms and in high society, as well as paederasty among *samurai* and monks. But one cannot compare this with the West, where many similar activities were probably expurgated from the records and there is no indication as to how widespread these practices were.

On the other hand, there were also the reactionary movements of Puritanism, such as the *samurai* meting out severe punishment for adultery in the Edo period and taking on many restrictions from the Christian West when Japan was trying to become a modern nation during the Meiji period.

In general the Japanese have far less inhibitions regarding sex than most other people. Cousins are allowed to marry each other. There are no circumcision rites. Female virginity or male chastity has less of the aura of saintliness than in the West. Masturbation and homosexuality do not have the stamp of deviationism. There is a festival to honour the male organ still being celebrated annually and in the eighties there was a boom in *mizuko jizo*, little Buddhist statues commemorating aborted foetuses.

The authorities apply the controls one would expect in any society but they seem to let the 'love hotels', with their offbeat contraptions, continue operating. They have banned publication of photographs which show pubic hair but do not stop the *Penthouse*-genre of magazines from publishing photographs of girls who have not reached puberty.

The truth probably is that the Japanese have not developed a basic social stance on sex and are letting it be as they do not rate it a matter of too much priority.

Romantic Love

One may get the impression from their social discipline that romantic love in the western sense of the expression is absent in Japan. It is not. Translations of the Mills and Boon and Harlequin type of romances sell like hot cakes in Japan.

It is difficult for a foreigner to understand their differentiation of sex and love. They themselves may have the same difficulty. As I mentioned earlier, one cannot see clearly defined lines of socially acceptable sexual behaviour.

Shinjinrui—*The New People*

Recently in Japan those who were born after 1960 have been called *shinjinrui*, literally, 'the new people'. This label was created by the older generation who in general believe that young adults today are a totally new breed of Japanese. Unlike the older generation, they have grown up in an environment of affluence and did not experience the war or the social turmoils and upheavals of the 1960s.

The older generation describe the characteristics of this new breed as self-centred, apathetic, action-oriented and irresponsible. *Shinjinrui* in general value individuality and privacy. They do not have the traditional respect for their seniors. They do not want to lead a life dominated by the company. They are reluctant to work overtime. And, in turn, they call the older generation 'the old type', *rojinrui*, and say they only live to work.

Shinjinrui women, like their male counterparts, embrace values quite different to what their mothers believed in. A 1984 opinion poll of single women showed that as much as 40% of the respondents thought it was not necessary to get married if they could be financially independent. It also revealed that more than half of the respondents wanted to continue working after marriage. They no longer accept their mothers' concept that the role of women is to serve others.

There is a definite parallel between 'Yuppie-ism' and the Japanese singles lifestyle. With no family obligations and no mortgage to pay for, working singles have a large purchasing power. Most of them are fashion-conscious and spend a considerable amount on clothes. Many have their own cars and are members of expensive sports clubs. Working women can usually afford to take more days off than men and make trips abroad regularly.

They do not have to save for weddings because the cost is usually carried by their parents. Weddings are a big business in Japan. On the average, a wedding ceremony can cost from US$10,000 to US$40,000. Rental of an 'all gold' wedding *kimono* can be as much as US$20,000.

The luxuries of the life of a single in Japan are pushing the marriage age up, beyond the traditional mid-20s for women and mid-to-late-20s for men. Even when they get married, *shinjinrui* prefer to lead a different married life from their parents. The DINK (Double Income No Kids) style of marriage is on the rise. One Dinker says that he and his wife do not have children because they put a priority on their own lives and that his wife works not because of money worries but because she wants to be financially independent.

Some social commentators say this is not true, and believe that the majority of *shinjinrui* revert to traditional lifestyles after a few years of marriage. This is why, they point out, there is no discernible change in Japanese social culture.

Japanese singles are less sexually active than in the West and singles seldom go to bars. They usually meet their prospective mates in college and at work, and tend to have longer-term relationships.

Matchmaking

For those who have missed opportunities to meet suitable partners, there is a matchmaking system to introduce eligible singles through a third party, usually a relative or friend of their parents. Today about one-third of the marriages in Japan are arranged through this system. Recently many companies using computers to match couples have sprung up. A typical company would charge US$2,000 for the service. Japan's largest matchmaking agency, Altmann, was reported in 1991 to have a pool of 26,000 members, each paying about US$3,700 in membership fees to enjoy the privilege of attending all the parties and outings organised by the agency. One company claims a 30% success rate, which is much higher than the supposed 10% rate of traditional matchmaking. Some users of the service feel that it is less embarrassing to screen many prospective mates because the introductions are made impersonally through the computer.

A rather brazen attempt to find brides has been carried out since 1989 by young farmers. Three bachelors representing about 70 in the Akita prefecture drove a tractor 700 km, taking five days to get to downtown Tokyo where they paraded with banners to entice young Tokyo women to be farmers' wives. The drift to the towns with all their city glamour is presenting big problems to young farmers. Up to October 1990, their success was only eight brides.

The Elderly

Japanese society is ageing faster than any other society in the world. Projections by the Health and Welfare Ministry indicate that the ratio of people aged 65 and over to total population will surpass that of any western society in the first half of the 21st century. In the mid-1980s, 10.3% of Japanese were 65 or older; this number was, at the time, 10% in the USA and over 15% in Sweden and West Germany. In 1998, 16% of the Japanese population were over 65.

The estimated lifespan in 2010 for males is 77.34 years, and for females, 83.37 years. The Japanese used to say, "A life lasts just 50 years." They now say, "A life lasts 80 years." Japanese business has started moving to satisfy the demands of the huge ageing population of the future. Cosmetics companies are looking at make-up for the elderly and the travel industry is organising special tours for them.

The people and the government are fully aware of the problems that the ageing population will bring and are increasingly and perhaps overly concerned about their life after retirement. At present, about 14% of annual income goes towards social security, medical insurance and pension payments, and about 15% is taken by national and local taxes. This is lower than the approximately 50% taken out of European and American salaries, and the Japanese government expects the people to bear a much larger financial burden for the elderly in the future. It also expects the private sector to assume a larger share of health, medical and welfare services.

People are saving more than before to prepare for their life after retirement. The Labour Ministry encourages workers to save at least 15 million yen (US$126,000) by the age of 65 to meet their retirement needs. Most salaried workers can expect to receive a monthly government pension equal to about 250,000 yen (US$2,100).

More than half of all Japanese companies have now adopted a mandatory retirement age of 60. The mandatory retirement age differs from industry to industry and from company to company. Many organisations are now helping retired workers to find new jobs.

Go *(a board game) competition organised for senior citizens in Japan.*

The most serious problem is caring for the elderly who are bedridden, senile or afflicted with Alzheimer's disease. In the past, it was always the family's responsibility to care for the elderly, but because of the severe housing shortage in urban Japan and the shift in social values which now favour the single-unit or nuclear family, carrying this responsibility is becoming increasingly difficult. Home care services for the elderly who live alone are in great demand; so are nursing homes for the elderly, but supply is not meeting these demands.

In 1986 the government tried to alleviate the problem of housing the elderly by promoting a plan to send senior people abroad, for example to villages in Spain. As many countries are exporting their pollution problems, Japan tried to export its 'oldies' problem. This idea met with a great deal of criticism and the government had to tone down its promotion of the scheme. The government is not just discussing the problem. It is seriously searching for alternative solutions.

Elderly Japanese want to remain active after retirement, especially the men, who have linked their whole lives and even their personal identities with their companies. Local authorities are offering various programmes to help the elderly enjoy a good life, such as *haiku* (poems of 17 syllables) lessons, sports events and outings to provide social contact. But, like people all over the world, what the elderly really want is to be with their children and grandchildren.

One interesting experiment is locating old people's homes next to kindergartens and using elderly people to help with the easier supervisory tasks while satisfying their desire to be with the young.

Religion

The Japanese are deeply religious, although this is not obvious. Some Japanese deny being religious, perhaps because they cannot see the difference between custom, superstition and religion. But religion plays a major role in their lives.

Shintoism, the way of the gods, is an integral part of Japanese life. It is not a religion with elaborate hierarchies of gods or profound precepts of the nature of divinity and man. It does not impose severe duties and rules on its adherents and does not call for special piety. But its rituals and tenets, a lot of which are animistic, permeate the Japanese character.

Buddhism is the main religion of Japan if we take Shintoism as something separate, as indeed it is. When Buddhism first came to Japan around the 6th century AD, via China and Korea, the question of whether there was conflict between Buddhism and Shintoism was resolved partly by Buddhist theologians viewing Shintoism as native beliefs of a lesser truth, in the long tradition of Buddhist tolerance.

The approximate distribution of Japanese professing the different religions is: Buddhism and Shintoism 106 million; Christianity nearly one million. A common, frivolous statement that the Japanese are born Shinto and die Buddhist describes the relative preference of rituals of birth and death, and says something about their attitudes to

Japanese write their requests on plaques and hang them on the wall.

the two religions.

State and Shintoism have been inextricably intertwined. General MacArthur and his administration tried to break this linkage with limited success. If anything, the merits of this link are greater than the disadvantages in Japan.

Christianity came to the south of Japan with the Portuguese and Spanish. They made sensational conversions and the intensity with which many converts plunged into their new faith is remarkable. It brought political problems. It is an interesting byroad not only of Japanese history but also of the aggressive spread of Christianity in the 16th century.

Variations within the Mass

This rough picture of the Japanese has assumed that there is a John Doe, the average man. The Japanese are in fact a homogeneous people, deviating less from the mean than most peoples, but there are individual and regional differences. It's time to describe some opinions the Japanese have of each other. Some are prejudices and some are wild generalisations, but they do indicate regional differences.

The Japanese say that in Hokkaido people treat each other as strangers. Unlike the people of Tohoku, they do not get away from their farms in winter to look for work but sit tight at home throughout the severe winter, braving the cold. They behave like westerners in demanding their rights and sticking to the rules.

Tohoku people are said to have been influenced by the gentle Ainu and are patient and can endure hardship. They are heavy sake drinkers. They have humility arising out of their relative poverty. So the talk goes.

Kanto – in which lies Tokyo, one of the centres of old *samurai* power and the ancient Imperial hub – is reputed to have people of strength who rate glory and honour more than money. Their dialect sounds are strong and harsh. For example, their word for stupid is *baka*, which is harsh and crisp, while stupid in Kansai is *aho*, a softer, kinder sound. Their stress is on social status and face-saving. There are other opinions. Kanto people believe they have the best cuisine, while Kansai people think they are crazy to not realise that man must eat only to live, and that money is really everything.

The Kanto image is of course complicated by Tokyo, the New York, the London, the Paris conurbation of the country. Within Kanto there is another set of pigeonholes. Kanagawa is progressive, Ibaragi is conservative, people of Gunma and Tochigi are more conservative yet also more volatile, Eichi people are manic-depressive …

In Kansai they are down-to-earth, putting money high on their list, frugal, but showy and extravagant when social occasions demand it. In Kansai the Osaka men look down on women more than anywhere else in Japan. They do business day and night. If you ask for directions from strangers they will direct you to the police box rather than waste time talking to you. We wonder if a lot of this comes from Tokyo talk.

Shikoku seems to have different types of people, depending on which part of Shikoku they come from. They vary from shrewd to reckless, optimistic and mild to money-hoarding and uncompromising.

Kyushu people are believed to be the best fighters. The island has produced some of the great entrepreneurs of Japanese business. Kyushu people are supposed to have a great desire to learn new things. They will stick to their principles and fight for them. They are Japan's Southerners who met the first waves of foreign intrusion.

It is a confusing patchwork of old-timer tales and possible traits arising out of their geography and history. You may have fun while you are in Japan proving or disproving some of these sweeping statements.

There is one group of Japanese who are the outcasts of society. They are a little blot on the face of Japan. The *Burakumin*. The Japanese themselves are extremely ashamed about these people today and it will cause a Japanese extreme discomfort if you raise the subject.

The *Burakumin* are completely Japanese in blood and in culture. There is nothing that will enable anyone who meets one of the *Burakumin* to distinguish her or him. These were the people who did the dirtiest tasks in the old days. They carried the nightsoil, tanned leather and butchered animals, which is anathema to Buddhism, and to Shintoism as well, with its stress on ritual purity. In most societies they would have been absorbed, and would have disappeared. But, with customary thoroughness, the mainstream Japanese resisted intermarriage with them, and they still exist today. One reason for checking bloodlines before a marriage is agreed to is to ensure that there is no *Burakumin* in the bride's or groom's ancestry.

They form less than 2% of the population. The word *Burakumin* is a shortened version of 'the hamlet people' or 'ghetto folk'.

There is another very small group of people in Japan who do not live together as a minority, and who have been forgotten except when they surface in entanglements with the police and in gruesome crime,

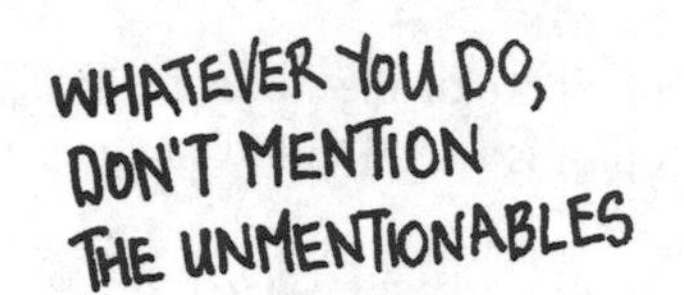

or as stars in the entertainment and fashion modelling world – the *konketsu*, mixed bloods. There are no statistics of them. The greater part of them are the products of the US occupation forces, and are now in their forties.

There are some ghastly stories of their rejection, some deeply moving stories of Japanese who have brought them up in the face of social antagonism and a few well known stories of success in the entertainment world. Their physiques and looks and their being different have given them something special.

Don't raise this subject either.

Do not confuse the *konketsu* with what the Japanese call *nisei*, the American-born Japanese, citizens of America who were imprisoned during the war by their own country. *Nisei* is also applied to second-generation Japanese migrants to the West and other countries. *Sansei* is the term for the third generation of Japanese living abroad.

The Japanese word for forgery, or something which is not the real thing, is *nise*. *Nisei* is literally second generation. Was this selected as an apt double-edged description?

Don't discuss *nisei* either.

SPECIAL DAYS

A Canadian friend of mine had Japanese buyers in Ottawa unexpectedly on Canada's big day, July 1st. He had promised to take his children to the national day fireworks display. He explained it to his Japanese visitors. Then they realised that from their hotel room high above the city they would have a superb view of the fireworks. They invited him and his family to come to the boss's room. My friend was delighted. It was a wonderful stroke of luck. The display and his children's reactions made it an extraordinary night.

When the fireworks display was at its height, the Japanese boss went quietly to his briefcase and took out his passport. He looked at it and uttered a cry of joy. "Hoi! It's my birthday today!"

My Canadian friend could see that it was not a contrived reaction. The man was truly surprised and overjoyed that it was his birthday. Richard and his wife couldn't understand it. The man didn't know his birthday?

We will now add to this chapter on the Japanese a few descriptive touches of events which are important to them. Like the Ramadan of Islam and Christmas of Christianity, such events reveal something about the culture.

New Year's Day

Their biggest day is New Year's Day. It used to be the first day of the lunar year but it is now fixed at the international calendar year, January 1st. A practical decision. It is a day of the family, of eating and drinking, dressing up and giving presents. *Oshogatsu* is New Year's Day and many Japanese still follow the old custom of counting their age from this day. So it is also a sort of birthday for many.

Preparations are made as the old year ends. There is a big cleaning-up at home, both inside and outside – the *osoji*. The traditional pine and bamboo decoration, *kado-matsu*, are put outside the house and the entrance is hung with twisted straw rope.

A young couple share a bite as they greet the New Year.

On New Year's Eve a visit to the local shrine is made to pray for good fortune in the coming year. A ceremony called the *oharai* frees believers from the old year's sins. Hands are clapped to bring the attention of the gods to the supplicants; arrows, votive tablets and talismans are offered, and coins are tossed into the offering bins.

At midnight the temple bells strike 108 times to usher in the New Year; 108 because there is a belief that man is born inheriting 108 evil desires that have to be driven away. (The Roman Catholics only have one Original Sin!) Some people go to the beaches and mountain tops to see the first sunrise of the year.

The people greet each other with "*Akemashite omedeto gozaimasu.*" Children get *otoshidama*, money gifts, in the morning and the adults open their New Year greeting cards.

The big meal is a huge breakfast which often extends to lunch. There are many special New Year dishes. There is the herring roe, *kazunoko*, a symbol of fertility and procreation; seven-herb rice porridge, *nanagusa-gayu*, for a healthy year ahead; rice cakes floating in a soup, *zoni*; the rich and elaborate *jyubako*, a heavy box with four tiers of solid food inside; and the series of sweet dishes, *kurikinton*, sweetened chestnuts mashed with sweet potatoes, and various rice cakes, *mochi*, stuffed with beans, *mamemochi* or adzuki bean jam, *anmochi* and many other *mochi*.

These days most Japanese spend the day in front of their television sets as the TV stations put on special New Year's Day programmes. But the traditional visiting is still being done and much sake is downed with the good wishes.

Climbing Mount Fuji

Climbing Fujisan would be an event in the life of any Japanese. Virtually every Japanese wants to climb Fujisan, and some climb it many times in spite of the proverb which says that only a fool climbs Mount Fuji more than once.

Mount Fuji is 3,776 metres high. The climb is a walking climb, but

is very strenuous and takes about ten hours. Two million people climb the mountain every year. Not all of them make it to the top; the last 1,500 metres is a stiff climb in a bleak setting of volcanic cinders without a blade of grass.

The name of the mountain comes from the Ainu phrase 'to burst forth'. The early Japanese named it after a relative of the sun goddess, Konohana-no-sakuya-hime, and thus connected to the rising sun, Mount Fuji evokes patriotic emotions. To watch the sun rise from Mount Fuji is something special to the Japanese.

There are mixed attitudes among the climbers. Some chant invocations to the goddess of the mountain. Some sing pop songs. Some joke and laugh. But all the time one hears the word of exhortation, *ganbatte*, press on!

All the practical necessities – food, drink, straw mats to lie on when you're tired – are there but do not seem to taint the atmosphere of the mountain.

Cherry Blossom Viewing or Hanami

The cherry flower has for centuries stirred Japanese poets and painters and viewing cherry trees in full bloom in the spring excites all

Hanami *is for everyone: the office picnic lunch crowd, the karaoke set, and even overnight campers.*

Japanese. Myriads of pinkish-white blossoms on rows and rows of trees in the parks, lining river banks, castle moats, lakes and open lawns make a truly beautiful sight.

The blossoms only last for about a week; the *samurai* saw in them a similarity to their own lives, that could end so suddenly, with their total commitment to their lords and masters. The first blossoms appear in Okinawa in February, and the flowering of cherry trees then spreads across the country, finally reaching Hokkaido in early May. The most famous viewing sites are Mount Yoshino near Kyoto, Ueno Park in Tokyo and Hirosaki in Amori prefecture.

Cherry blossom viewing is not just enjoyed by aesthetes and lovers of nature. It is an activity that all of Japan rushes into with much gusto. There are sedate viewers, lovers holding hands, and lively groups singing, laughing loudly and raucously, dancing, and generally letting themselves go with an abandon one would never expect after seeing them hunched over their desks and machines in offices and factories.

Travel

The Japanese have become great travellers. Leisure travel is a huge business.

One curious result of this was reported in the magazine *PHP* in 1990. The last shoeshine operator at Narita airport packed up in 1990. With typical Japanese thoroughness, a reporter of *Asahi Shimbun*, who saw the implications of this, hid under a staircase at the airport and conducted what he called a 'low level survey', observing the shoes of passers-by. He logged his observations faithfully. They showed that sneakers and informal shoes have become the order of the day for Japanese travellers. Polished leather has gone. Leisure travel had surpassed business travel.

THINGS JAPANESE

We continue this chapter on the Japanese by describing some objects which are part and parcel of the Japanese lives and which you will come across again and again. In many ways they reflect the Japaneseness of the users. Physical things like clothing, utensils, buildings, materials and mechanisms used by people in any country reflect not just the state of a civilisation, but also the nature of a culture that adopted them, and that has in turn been influenced and restricted by them. During the industrial revolution two hundred years ago the availability of Indian cotton to the working classes – softer than stiff woollen fabrics, and falling gently on curves of the female form – and the new dyes with their bright striking colours caused new drifts in the social systems of Europe. Physical objects and the psyche of man are in constant conflict, balance and interaction.

Furoshiki

The *furoshiki* is a cloth in which the Japanese wrap a great variety of objects. It is their 'holdall' in the full sense of the word.

It is the simplest carrying device one can imagine and through all the years of development of containers and cases the basic *furoshiki* still survives in Japan. In spite of their elaborate packaging for gifts, the down-to-earth *furoshiki* is the first thing a Japanese would think of if he has to carry something or a collection of things. When you have seen the zillion uses of the ubiquitous *furoshiki*, you will not be surprised if an executive comes into the office one day with a *furoshiki* instead of his standard briefcase!

Geta

Geta are wooden clogs.

Compared to Dutch and Chinese clogs, it is interesting how the Japanese arrived at a different design for the same purpose of keeping their feet clean and dry and protecting the soles from harsh ground at a minimum cost. They are usually 5 cm high but *amageta* – *geta* for the rain – can be 7–10 cm high.

On the one hand the *geta* raise feet well above the ground, better than other clogs, but on the other hand, throughout the ages, they have not corrected a basic flaw. The strap which goes between the big toe and the second toe is not in the right position as it is with today's thongs or flip-flops (or *surripa* in Japanese). It is in the centre of the clog. If you keep your feet pointing straight ahead wearing *geta*, the *geta* will have to point inwards, giving you a knock-kneed appearance.

Note that at a Japanese *ryokan* or *minshoku* (inn) you will have slippers to wear in your room, but when you go to the bathroom there will be *geta* there for you. It is part of the Japanese finickiness about the feet being a source of dirt and their narrow solutions to many problems. In the bedroom, slippers; and in the wet areas, *geta*.

Geta are not just for everyday wear. They are also used for traditional formal occasions. *Geta* for men are of plain wood with black straps, but women use lacquered black or vermillion *geta* with colourful straps of velvet or silk.

Hachimaki

This is the headband that you see Japanese workers wearing. It is used when one is involved in strenuous work. It keeps the sweat away from the eyes, but it also has a symbolic function. It tells everyone that you are busy and should not be disturbed. It has a hint of professionalism. The men wearing *hachimaki* at festivals are not just sightseers but members of the working team. Identical *hachimaki* identify the team in different situations. Students used to wear *hachimaki* when rioting and political demonstrators wear them today to show that they are dead serious and not fooling around.

Apart from the external effect, tying on the *hachimaki* brings on the attitude of girding one's loins to exert one's best. Students wear a *hachimaki* in the quiet of their rooms when studying for examinations. Pilots during the war wore *hachimaki* in the isolation of their cockpits.

It is not just a dirty-looking towel. It is a Japanese thing in tune with their approach towards life in general.

Jinjya

The *jinjya* is a Shinto shrine. As we explained above, the Japanese treat Shintoism as something separate from Buddhism and see no conflict in following both faiths. That's why some statistics show 106 million Shinto believers and 106 million Buddhists – which add up to almost twice the total population!

The *jinjya* houses a divine natural spirit, a *kami*, which can be loosely translated as a god. The sanctuary for the *kami* is in the centre of the shrine, called the *haiden*. You will not be allowed into the *haiden*.

The *torii* is the main gateway arch which isolates the shrine from the outside world. But it is not a closed door; it sets up a symbolic line. The *torii* is sometimes quite far from the shrine itself. This allows visitors time to compose themselves before they reach the shrine.

Torii were originally bird perches on which live cocks, offerings to the sun goddess, Amaterasu, were placed by worshippers. *Torii* always have four horizontal lines. Three are often straight and the fourth bowed in a soft curve.

The *jinjya* is always a simple structure, unlike some of the elaborate Buddhist temples. In the grounds you will see *ishidoro*, stone lanterns, *komainu*, stone statues of dog-lions and wooden tablets inscribed with requests to the gods. There will also be a *mizuya*, the water basin for purification of the hands and the mouth.

Shrines are usually located in places of natural beauty, or in isolated places, because the Japanese believe that these locations will please the gods. Mountains, hilltops and rises are common sites. There are, however, numerous miniature shrines all over the country where special events have occurred, which may seem to you sites that would not please any tolerant, easygoing god.

Shrines face the south and sometimes the east. But never the unlucky west or north.

Pachinko

The Japanese took to the American pinball machine years ago and made it part of their urban lifestyle. They have clung to this mindless contraption that met certain wants in the West in the days when simple entertainments gave satisfaction. It is a postwar craze. It may be significant that just after the war the *pachinko* parlours used to play the Imperial Navy March loudly.

This is a strange paradox of modern Japan. It is unbelievable that people who throw their whole selves into their work or their artistic pursuits, into their passions of golf or *sumo* or religious self-immolation, can waste so much time on *pachinko*. *Pachinko* parlours are everywhere. Millions play the machines. Some do it just to kill time.

Gambling or hope for a fortune is not the draw as the prizes are meagre. It is a harmless escapism.

Behind the bright lights and the loud music of *pachinko* parlours are the struggles of the *yakuza* gangsters for control; the *kugishi*, literally nail-men, who move in every night to adjust key nails, check the weights of the balls and apply scientific knowledge and empirical skills to keep the odds within profitable limits; and the *pachinko* parlour operator's secret list of ex-*kugishi* who are banned by the parlours. There are even magazines, very much like computer magazines, devoted to the techniques of *pachinko* and how to score in the game.

This is another face of Japan.

Kami, *Paper*

Paper is a material that has always been interleaved into the fabric of Japanese living. You have heard of their 'paper houses', actually timber frames with paper infilling. And the paper-folding art of *origami* and *kirie*, pictures of cut paper, are two examples of the use of paper that the Japanese seem to have exploited more than any other country.

Handmade paper was in use in Japan centuries before Europe saw its possibilities. Paper is still a material they appreciate and respect today. You will see paper strips in almost every shrine and temple. You will notice the fancy foldings, the different textures and patterns of their gift wraps.

Some of the uses are disappearing. Paper was used for many everyday requirements before the war: infilling of *fusuma*, sliding doors, oiled paper in umbrellas, raincoats, fireworks, and even a *kimono* known as *kamiko*. A well known picture of a *kimono* which an ardent lover presented to his lady shows that it is made of paper strips, each with a poem of passionate love on it.

Paper was used in a major war project. Huge 9.9 metre balloons filled with hydrogen gas were fabricated from handmade paper to take advantage of a high altitude jet-stream. Nine thousand balloons were launched and an estimated one thousand dropped their bomb loads in America. American security clapped a news blackout on these 'balloon bombs' because, although the damage they could do was negligible, their effect on morale would have been significant.

In the old days the main production of the fine handmade papers, *washi*, was by farmers in the winter. It was a fortuitous arrangement of nature that the leaves of the paper mulberry tree, the *kozo*, would start falling when the harvesting work-peak was over and the trees could be cut for paper-making. Paper-making by hand reached its peak in the middle of the 1800s and started to fall away with the arrival of modern paper-making machines.

The appreciation of paper is an indication of Japanese sensitivity to texture, of their striving for perfection, and of a past which, though fading, will leave its traces for at least one more generation.

Kimono *and* Yukata

Kimono, literally a thing to wear, came to Japan from China as an undergarment in the 7th century. In the 12th and 13th centuries it became an elaborately decorated outer garment, and the *kimono*'s final acceptance was when the *samurai* adopted it in the 14th century.

With the kimono *comes the* obi, *the waist band, changing with the seasons and carefully selected to be in harmony with the age of the wearer.*

The *shogunate* actually passed laws to prohibit the masses from wearing *kimono* but the nouveau riche Edoites, *geisha* and other entertainers began wearing them and control became impossible.

The *kimono* is a most impractical garment. Just as the courts in Europe punished themselves with Grecian bends and tightened waists, the Japanese bore the discomfort to look beautiful by their standards of the day. The pornographic Hokusai prints of making love between layers of *kimono* cloth are just one indication of the impracticality of the *kimono*. The *kimono* is not just one garment. It is a series of layers of silk with all sorts of complicated tying strings.

Yet the *kimono* is a beautiful thing. Today Japanese women only wear *kimono* at special events such as at *Oshogatsu*, for visits to shrines, at weddings, graduation receptions and funerals. Still clinging to the past.

The *kimono* in its modern functional form, known as the *yukata*, is still very much a part of Japanese life. It is another example of the Japanese coming to a solution by finding the mean between the extremes. The cut of the *kimono* is still there but the *yukata* is one of the most comfortable forms of dress in the humid summer or in a heated hotel room. And it is acceptable in the street at hot spring resorts.

Manga, *Comics*

There is a madness about *manga* in Japan. It started in the early 20th century when ideas poured in from the West. It fitted in with the humorous and ribald Japanese woodblock prints, their often crude *senryo* poems, and comic stage entertainment. In the mid-sixties *manga* took off, and it is now a major sector of the publishing industry, with many *manga* hitting over a million copies a month. The contents are diverse; from old *samurai* and *ninja* tales and educational publications to some of the coarsest and most brazenly sexual stories, with sadism and masochism that would not pass any television censor.

You will see people reading *manga* everywhere in Japan. Restaurants provide a bookshelf of *manga* for people dining alone. On more than one occasion I have seen from an elevated vantage point, truck drivers snatching glances at *manga* open on the seat beside them.

In 1983 a critical book on *manga*, entitled *Manga, Manga!* became a controversial bestseller. The writer defended *manga* as a necessary escape from the pressures of Japanese life. He said that it was not *manga* that was causing the drop in reading in Japan, but

television. He was an American graduate of a Japanese language school, Frederick Schodt.

Ofuro, *the bath*

The bath is an essential part of Japanese life. Their Shinto rituals stressed purification and cleanliness. Bathing in an icy cold stream or under a waterfall was part of the ritual necessary before entering a Shinto shrine. Even today, having a bath is treated by many as the essential preliminary cleansing before participating in *matsuri*, festivals.

The Japanese soak themselves in extremely hot water up to their necks in heated large tubs. The best baths, the old-timers will tell you, are those made of cypress wood. It is a sensation that they enjoy tremendously. It relaxes the body after a day of tension at work.

Initiating their gaijin *friends into the* ofuro.

They clean themselves meticulously before they go into the bathtub because the same water is either used by the whole family in turn or, if it is big enough, together at the same time. There is a conventional sequence which dictates that the father goes in first, followed by the sons and then the women of the family. If there are servants, they go in last. The father would go in after dinner at about 7 p.m. and he could take 40 minutes. The last one would get out of the bathtub as late as 11:30 if it was a large family. If you are staying at a small inn or at a friend's house and you are asked to have your bath, do not take it as a slight. It is an honour to go in first.

In the countryside, in the old days, three or four families would pool their firewood resources by bathing at each house in turn. In a way it was a very informal social event with the adults sitting around in their light evening *kimono* drinking tea and talking while awaiting their turn.

Note that the word for 'bath' has, in front of it, the honorific *o*, which is not relegated to objects or ceremonies lightly.

Tatami

The *tatami* is a floor mat. Its widespread use in Japan reflects some facets of the Japanese character.

As life got more complicated in the 20th century, standards were set up everywhere to simplify producers meeting users' needs. One fundamental standard was never developed in the West: the standard of living space. In Japan the 3 by 6 foot *tatami* is the basic standard of floor space. The Japanese don't have to imagine a, say, 4 by 2.5 metre room, or a 12 by 9 foot room if houses are being discussed. The number of *tatami* gives them the space concept at once.

Japanese architecture never forgets its functional objective of housing the human being, whether for sleeping or working. The *tatami* helps them to keep relating all plan areas to the space needed for a human to lie down comfortably. In the earlier days Japanese architects could not accept the metre as a measure because it did not seem to relate to the human frame, and used the foot, but rejected inches and changed them to decimals of a foot.

The *tatami* was not always a standard. In the Heian period (794–1185) the size of the *tatami* was determined by the rank of the man who sat on it. The lowest ranking members of the court sat on the bare floor. The size was standardised sometime during the Ashikaga period (1333–1573).

Tatami are made of tightly woven rice straw and covered with a woven rush. The edges are bound with cotton. They are firm but resilient. They yield to the shape of one's foot and creak softly. They absorb and release moisture depending on the ambient humidity and thus help to condition the air in the room to some extent. When new, they exude a pleasant aroma which one writer has described as 'the sweet smell of straw in the morning'.

There is an old Japanese saying, "The *tatami*, like a wife, is best when new." They used to change them every spring in the old days (the *tatami*, not the wives).

Are the Japanese Changing?

Yes, they are.

That's the simple answer but there are so many questions which spin off from there. No one has the full answer. In this book, only the author's subjective views can be given, but they will provide you with starting points to stimulate your interest in the Japanese and develop your own thoughts while you live in Japan.

What about their rigid social codes?

It's doubtful that this will ever change. There will be changes to the unwritten social laws, but the norm will still be sought by every Japanese. It is part of their group psyche.

It's been said that the Japanese developed strict rules of living

Punk is in among Japanese teenagers.

because they are a very emotional people and the only way they could live together is by laying down the law, like the military, which has to cope with a wide range of individuals and forge them into a single force. Their tendency to form groups and their behavioural codes are chicken and egg elements of the society. The Japanese will, most likely, preserve the fundamental fabric.

Will they continue to think that they are poor?

No. This is a key question.

It has been suggested above that the drive to rise out of their poverty was one of the engines of their growth. If there is no external enemy, or stimulus, the forces binding them together against the world will be severely weakened.

The belief that they are a poor nation will be eroded fairly quickly, but the Japanese will find other goals to push themselves towards and these will continue to keep them the Japanese they are today – with closed ranks facing a foreign world.

It is difficult to predict these new stimuli. One thought: the USA led the human race in its breaking into outer space. This once stirred the hearts of all Americans. If Japan had been in that position, the conquest of outer space would have been a huge national driving force. In a way, it's as if your brother was Neil Armstrong.

There are already signs that their workaholic lifestyle is slipping.

Yes. They are relaxing. There are reports of salesmen goofing off at *pachinko* and *go* parlours. Unions are asking for more leisure time. And although they do not watch the clock, there is a lot of wasted time in the offices. The Swedish study of time spent at work and leisure (see page 25) shows that the Japanese are really not very far in front of other developed nations in the allocation of living time. As in so many countries, immigrant labour has been creeping in to do the dirty work. The facts are there.

The Japanese are definitely beginning to sit back. So is the rest of the world. It is really a question of relative workaholism.

But doesn't their workaholic philosophy also embody so many other things like Puritanism which built the United States of America, Scotland, Holland, and other countries?
Yes. But they will not throw out everything with the bath water. The 'greening of America' pointed out similar silver linings when the world was looking only at the dark storm clouds.

Their large national savings will not change; leisure travel does not eat too much into it. Neither will their propensity to think long-term in business, even if Japan adopts a four-day working week.

Aren't the* shinjinrui *lifestyles significant?
The *shinjinrui* should not be read as a major indicator, because after a few years of marriage they usually cease to be *shinjinrui*.

Japanese children are changing. They will change the society.
Not necessarily. The school systems will not change significantly. The elders continue to dictate policy, unlike on the American continent and in some newly developed countries in Asia. Look back to the postwar years of the students' and the communists' bid for power. Those petered out fairly quickly.

What then is the major force that will change Japanese society?
The women. It's something like the serfs of feudal society and the proletariat of France boiling up into an explosion of revolution. These suppressed forces will not erupt like their volcanoes. But it is not like the silent resentment of non-white Africans in South Africa or the impotent dissatisfaction of the low castes in India. The women in Japan have developed as much as their men. Only, by and large, they are still traditionalists.

Imagine a scenario all over the country of the working woman slowly and gently making her 'cockroach husband' play a bigger role at home. The Japanese marriage contract is out of date. Their media keeps saying this in many different ways, and the message is slowly getting through.

Divorces will increase. Not because of a new laxity in marital morals, but because the redistribution of domestic power will bring more unhappiness than a *kateinai rikon* can contain. It won't be the other woman, but the first woman, once known as 'the one inside', *inside* meaning behind the screens.

Some may not agree. Read what follows from *The Japanese Mind* by Robert C. Christopher (1984, Pan Books) – then decide for yourself.

> "A great many westerners, probably the majority of them, live in an illusion that the Japanese male is lord of all he surveys. In fact this has not been the case for a long time.
>
> "There is a perfectly good Japanese word for hen-pecked – *kaka danka* – and it is not one of recent coinage. Consider for example the case of former Prime Minister Takeo Miki, whose wife once publicly proclaimed that her man 'hardly knows how to wash his face properly' and on another occasion felt obliged to assure an interviewer that she had never struck Miki."

The ageing society?

There is no doubt that this will become a major factor in social change. But there are no precedents to guide us. There are reports of increased crime by the elderly, and more suicides.

— *Chapter Three* —

SETTLING DOWN IN JAPAN

Sooner or later you will have to get down to organising the basic necessities of living – food, shelter, clothing – and the many other needs of modern life such as transport, education, banking, medical and dental care, etc.

The Japanese have a combination of three words for the basic necessities of food, shelter and clothing. It is *i-shoku-ju*: clothing-food-shelter. Note the order. To the Japanese, clothing, the external appearance, comes first. Housing is last. You will discover that the Japanese are always well dressed and eat reasonably well, but their standards of housing are well below those of the West. There is a desperate shortage of housing, and rents and mortgage rates are very high.

In this chapter you will be guided through some of these matters. There is, however, no substitute for a 'resource person' or friend and our first piece of advice is that you try to find one.

A Japanese who speaks English will not only be able to help you with the facts and the language, but with him or her by your side it will be much easier to win the trust of landlords, doctors, bank clerks and officials of the local authorities. Personal introductions make such a difference to the Japanese. Besides that, you will learn the little things that you never thought of asking and he or she never thought of telling you as you go around with your guide in the first few days.

Businessmen would probably be able to find such a person at their office. Expatriate wives who have been through it all will give invaluable advice, but there is no better guide than a Japanese.

Commercial organisations provide such services. Two of them are:

• Oak Associates – Ask for either their free 'Welcome Furoshiki' home visit service or their family orientation programmes. (*Furoshiki* is a bundle, a package.)

• Culture Shock – As their name implies, they offer a variety of services to help visitors and expatriates cope with initial culture shock.

The telephone numbers of both are given in Chapter 9.

On Arrival

The immigration procedures are fairly standard. You have to complete the embarkation/disembarkation card and present this with your passport, which should have a visa in it, and the immigration officer will mark your legal period of stay in Japan on the card. Note that although the Japanese as a rule have very few restrictions on smoking, you would be considered rude if you smoked while standing in front of the immigration counter.

"Keep in mind that the Lingua Franca here is Japanese, and unless you have already studied the language you'll be hamstrung from day one. The language barrier will be a constant reminder in every facet of your daily life, from buying tomatoes to getting a haircut. At first it's fun; after six months, it's just frustrating."
—*SWET Newsletter*, November 1988

It is important for expatriates who leave Japan temporarily to get a re-entry permit from the Regional Immigration Office. You should go in person, bringing your passport, Alien Registration Certificate (see below) and re-entry form. Remember also that if you have to extend your stay, you must report in person to the Immigration Bureau at least two weeks before visa expiration, presenting your passport with a written statement of reasons for extension. A fee has to be paid for both re-entry and extension applications. Staying in Japan beyond the permitted period or re-entering the country without a permit will get you into a lot of trouble.

If you do have problems with the immigration official, raising your voice, thumping the desk and demanding to see the top man is the worst thing you could do in Japan. This is not just for the immigration and customs people. Everywhere in the country a show of aggressiveness is regarded as the height of rudeness.

At Narita International Airport help on arrival is available from the Tourist Information Centre at both airport terminals, or by telephoning (0476) 30-3383 (Narita) or (03) 3201-3331 (Tokyo).

Help by telephone is also available from Teletourist Service, Japan Guide Association and JATA (Japanese Association of Travel Agents). For emergencies, call TELL (Tokyo English Life Line), Agape House, or Japan Helpline. See Chapter 9 for all numbers. The coins needed for public telephones are also given in that chapter.

The average rate for guides or interpreters is 12,000–15,000 yen (US$100–125) a day, in addition to transport costs, meals and accommodation for the duration of the assignment. Compare this with business interpreters whose rates range from 30,000 to 75,000 yen (US$250–630) a day. In April 1990, Japan introduced 'goodwill guides', identifiable by the badge they wear. This service is provided *at no charge* and is especially useful for foreigners at train stations, in shops, and on streets everywhere. Goodwill guides are present also at the Asakusa Tourist Centre, JR Kyoto Station, Osaka Station and all tourist information offices.

If you arrive ill, there is a clinic in the first basement of the central wing of the airport building. For 'Lost and Found' contact the information counter on the first floor (ground floor) or the service counter on the third floor.

The Tokyo International Airport is located about 60 kilometres outside Tokyo, one to two hours away. There are Airport Limousine buses which leave the airport every 10–15 minutes and stop at major hotels. Luggage is no problem with this service. It stops at midnight. The bus ends its 70-minute run in downtown Tokyo at the Tokyo City Air Terminal (TCAT) at Hakozai. There is also a 70-minute shuttle train service, the Keisei Skyliner, from the airport to Ueno Station. If you have a lot of luggage the Skyliner is not recommended. There are taxis, of course, but be prepared to pay at least 30,000 yen (US$250).

If you have come to Japan to stay, you must report to the local ward office to get an Alien Registration Certificate within 90 days of your arrival for all members of your family. This certificate must be carried on your person while you are in Japan. The procedures are slightly different for children below age 16.

"Even if you do the paperwork right the first time, you may have to apply for a visa extension as often as every six months. Job changes – whether circumstances justify them or not – are likely to prejudice your chances with immigration authorities for a longer stay."

SWET Newsletter,
November 1988

Clothing

You should buy your clothes at home before you come to Japan, for size is a problem. Even if you find a size that fits you, the sleeves may be shorter and the hips narrower than the same Caucasian size. This problem also applies to underwear, shoes, socks and hosiery.

In spring and fall, when the weather is mild and crisp, you will need light sweaters and shirts and a light coat. The summers are hot and very humid, calling for cotton and linen with short sleeves for informal occasions. Leave all your very brief shorts and bare midriff clothes at home, unless you want to wear them only in your apartment. The Japanese rarely wear tank-tops or very brief shorts in public, even when it is sizzling hot. You will stand out like a sore thumb if you appear in public showing too much flesh.

You need a raincoat. There is a month of rain in May–June.

In winter the temperature in Tokyo drops down to 23°F (–5°C). There are no blizzards and in the major cities heavy snowfall is rare but you still need a heavy winter coat and jacket and warm woollen clothes. A heavy suit for men and a thick dress for social evenings for women is recommended. And don't forget warm socks. If you are invited to a Japanese house, you will be sitting around in your socks and the floor will most probably not be heated.

In the cities, you will have to do a lot more walking because of the traffic congestion and parking difficulties. So make sure you have good walking shoes. Neckties, belts and other accessories are also smaller in Japan. Bring what you need with you.

Women will find the finest designer clothes in Tokyo, but the size and shape problem will come up again. So will price problems. Earrings for pierced ears are difficult to find.

The general tone of dressing in Japan is formal. Even on occasions when you would expect more casual wear, they will be formally dressed. You cannot be wrong if you over-dress rather than under-dress. The style in the cities is European, or American. *Kimono* have disappeared from everyday life. They are only worn at special traditional functions these days.

In business situations smart clothing is essential. But the average Japanese businessman does not attempt to be up-to-date in fashion. He aims at the styles of the American politician or the British city businessman.

Teenagers do not dress down as they do in the West. You rarely see young people in rugged, torn or worn clothes, except perhaps in Harajuku on a Sunday. In fact, many young Japanese are quite fashion-conscious and wear designer clothes.

There is a good variety of children's clothes in Japan. Girls tend to be dressed more in skirts than in pants. Boys are often in short pants all year round.

Although you are advised to bring what you need from home, shopping for clothes in Japan is not hopeless. There are stores, advertised in the English periodicals, that carry extra-large sizes in clothes and shoes, as young Japanese are bigger and taller than their parents. Their range is, however, narrow. There are also up-market designer wear boutiques which carry larger sizes for Caucasians. Tailored clothes are expensive. It may be cheaper to fly to Hong Kong with your pattern books to get a dress or a suit made!

If the Japanese sizes do fit you, go to the end-of-summer and winter sales. Leave your name and address at your favourite department stores and they will mail information about their sales to you.

You may want to buy a traditional *kimono*. It would cost you anywhere between 200,000 yen (US$1,700) to 1,000,000 yen (US$8,000). Second-hand kimonos are available at a tenth of the price. Consider buying the lighter summer *kimono*, the unisex *yukata*, which are light and comfortable to wear and are reasonably priced around 5,000 yen (about US$40) or even less. Many hotels sell their own *yukata* which are usually available in larger sizes.

Japanese, US and European Sizes

WOMEN'S CLOTHES

Japan	7(S)	9(M)	11(L)	13(XL)
USA	3	4–5	5–6	7–8
Bust (inches)	32	34	36	38
Europe (cm)	80	86	91	102

SHIRTS

Japan, Europe	36	37	38	39/40	41	42	43	44
USA/UK	14	14.5	15	15.5	16	16.5	17	17.5

SHOES

Japan	23.5	24	24.5	25	25.5	26	26.5	27	27.5
USA	5.5	6	6.5	7	7.5	8	8.5	9	9.5
Europe	37	37.5	38	38.5	39	39.5	40	40.5	41

If you are a businesswoman you have first of all to be aware that you could overwhelm the Japanese male with your appearance. They are not used to glamour in the executive suite. Play down your make-up, jewellery and accessories. But don't forget the quality-consciousness prevalent in Japan. They will recognise up-market jewellery and accessories. Trousers, teenage styles, plunging necklines, brazen bare backs and split skirts will rock them. So will way-out hairdos, especially if you're over 40. High heels may make you appear to tower over them.

There are many broad-minded men in executive positions today who will be charmed by the *gaijin* woman who's different, but if you haven't met or sized up your contact, stick to the old sober tones and go and look for that brown suit you abandoned years ago; but check if it still fits before you pack it!

> "Be prepared for high prices. Translated into your national currency, costs for food, daily necessities and housing are probably exorbitant and are getting higher."
>
> —*SWET Newsletter*, November 1988

Buying Food

You will find most of the staple western foods in Japan – meat, potatoes, bread, milk, vegetables, eggs and fruit. Butter, cheese, coffee, tea and cereals are also available. There are supermarkets which cater for the international community and stock a wider selection of western foods than Japanese supermarkets. But food prices will shock you.

Beef is exorbitantly expensive. It is sold by the 100 g, not by pounds and ounces. Chicken and pork are reasonably priced. Frozen meat is not common and neither are whole chickens or turkeys. Turkeys can only be obtained from special stores.

Seafood is abundant and always fresh. Fish is one of the main sources of protein for the Japanese and large quantities are sold. Fish and other seafood are therefore relatively cheap.

Many fish familiar to an American or European are available – tuna, mackerel, sea bream, sardine, herring – though some are slightly different to what you may be familiar with, like the salmon-trout (a variety of trout) or the *sanma* (a kind of mackerel). There are also fish which you may not know, and which are worth trying; if you do try them, ask how they are usually cooked.

Fish sold for *sashimi* or *sushi* (dishes with raw fish) cost a lot more and are not worth buying for cooking. Many of the vegetables and fruit grown in North America and Europe are found in Japan: cabbage, lettuce, french beans, sweet beans, carrots, potatoes, spinach, even beetroot, squash and brussels sprouts. Some vegetables are imported – artichoke and zucchini, for example.

There are, however, many Japanese products that are close to vegetables you know. The *daikon* is one. It is a kind of turnip or radish which the Japanese use as a vegetable – boiled, pickled or in stews – and as a seasoning. Finely sliced, it not only tastes good with *sashimi* but also looks pretty and delicate. Mushrooms are another example. You may be familiar with the *shiitake*. You should try the others.

Many of the herbs and spices you use at home are not imported into Japan. Try their herbs and garnishings which often have flavours approximating the ones you know. If you love the good old tastes of home, drop into the international stores, which are importing more spices and herbs these days.

Both imported fruit and local fruit are sold everywhere, but fruits that are bought as gifts, like musk-melons, are extremely expensive (5,000–10,000 yen or US$40–80 each). Avocado is imported and is reasonably priced. Japanese apples are delicious, but can cost as much as 150 to 300 yen each (US$1.25 – 2.50). There is a fruit called *nashi* that looks like an apple but tastes like a pear. There are strawberries and other berries but not in as many varieties as in Europe or North America. You should try the Japanese tangerine, the *mikan*, which is relatively cheap, and of course, you must try *sakuranbo*, the Japanese cherries.

Snack shops have all the familiar features of burger shops everywhere.

Bread is generally not as good in Japan as overseas. The range is limited. The international supermarkets have a wider variety.

Cream cheese and Parmesan cheese are about the only two kinds of cheese one sees in Japan. Some stores may have imported Brie or Camembert but you will generally have to live with a limited range of cheese. Milk in Japan may taste a little different to you. This is because pasteurisation is carried out at higher temperatures in Japan than elsewhere. A lower temperature pasteurised milk is now available at some stores.

Have a look at what Japanese housewives are buying. The basement of any department store stocks an amazing variety of food. Many counters have small sample pieces for you to try. Look at the whole range of *tofu*, the soybean cake, which is another major source of protein for the Japanese, and the seaweeds, *wakame* and *nori*, which are rich in calcium, vitamin A, iron and iodine.

If these foods interest you, there are many Japanese cookbooks available. And if you want to have a good look at what the Japanese buy, go to the huge wholesale food market at Tsukiji in Tokyo.

If shopping for food is really important to you, get a copy of *A Guide to Food Buying in Japan* by Carolyn R. Krouse. And if you get really stuck don't forget that there may be a fast-food place round the corner – Kentucky Fried Chicken, McDonald's, Pizza Hut, Baskin-Robbins, Dunkin' Donuts. The list gets longer every year.

Housing – Temporary

Various types of temporary accommodation which will allow you to take your time choosing a house or apartment to rent on a lease can be obtained in most cities. Try to book even temporary housing before you leave home. The Japanese Tourist Information Service can assist you in finding accommodation if you do arrive and find yourself stranded without a reservation. (See p. 71.)

Hotel rates range from about 7,000 yen (US$60) for 'capsule' hotels to 40,000 yen (US$340) per person per night, the rates rising steeply skyward as the star ranking goes up. But there are 'business hotels' in most cities that average about 10,000 yen (US$85).

Note that the rates quoted here are the basic rates. To this a 10% government tax and usually a 10% service charge are added. There is no tipping in Japanese hotels and restaurants.

The other alternative is the Japanese-style inn, the *ryokan*. A *ryokan* will have Japanese-style rooms with *tatami* and *futon*, bedding that is spread out each night and put away in the morning, sliding doors and a Japanese bath. You are given slippers when you arrive and you leave your shoes at the door. You are also given a light *yukata* to wear while you are there. The service in these places is usually excellent but you may have to struggle with your limited Japanese and sign language.

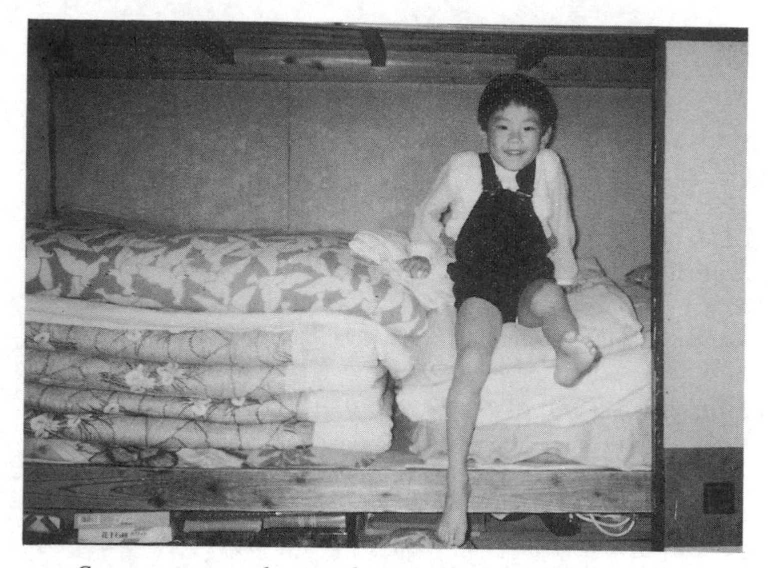

Compact rooms are kept neat by storing futon *behind sliding doors.*

The rates for good *ryokans* are about 15,000 yen (US$126) per person per night, usually with breakfast included. There are cheaper Japanese inns known as *minshuku* all over the country, similar to the European pensions in standard but Japanese in style. *Minshuku* rates are in the region of 7,000 yen upwards (US$60) per person per night.

For those on tight budgets there are youth hostels that cost about 3,000 yen (US$17–25). Information on youth hostels can be obtained from Japan Youth Hostels Inc, Suidobashi Nishiguchi Kaikan, 2-20-7 Misaki-cho, Chiyoda-ku, Tokyo 101-0061, tel: (03) 3288-1417, 1424, (03) 3288-0260 (Travel), fax: (03) 3288-1248, 3288-1490 (Travel), email: jyh@znet.or.jp. Foreigners on shoestring budgets can also check into economy lodges – 40,000 yen (US$335) a week, or even a month for some – until they find more permanent housing.

If you are really adventurous, many temples offer simple lodging and breakfast for about 2,500 yen (US$21). The temples request their guests to rise early and make their contribution to the temple, in addition to the lodging fee, with some small task such as sweeping the garden or partaking in their activities by meditation, *zazen*.

The brave may want to consider the 'love hotels' which are very comfortable and reasonably priced at 10,000–12,000 yen (US$85–100) a night. They are often sensationally decorated, and equipped with a television, private shower and bath facilities and sometimes even a vibrating bed to massage you into soothing sleep!

Furnished apartments known as 'apartment hotels' are also available for periods from a week to a few months. Costs are around 180,000 yen (US$1,500) a month.

Housing – Long-term

Types of Housing

Houses and apartments are described in advertisements as 1DK, 2LDK, etc. D stands for dining room, L for living room, K for kitchen. The numeral stands for the number of bedrooms. Hence, 3LDK is a 3-bedroom lodging with a living-cum-dining room and a kitchenette. A few of the smaller early *apato* built immediately after the war do not have a bathroom. A public bath, however, is often located near by.

There are three types of housing: *apato* (Japanese English for apartment), mansion and house.

Apato are apartments located in two-storey houses, often wooden. It is the cheapest type of rented accommodation, usually with one- or two-*tatami* (see below) rooms, a kitchen, a bathroom and a toilet. Cheaper *apato* have shared toilets and no bathrooms; tenants use the nearest public bathhouse. In Tokyo reasonable *apato* rents are about 70,000 yen (US$600) a month.

Mansions are higher-grade apartments in concrete framed buildings of over three stories. Typically, they have both Japanese and western-style rooms and a kitchen, a bathroom and a toilet. There are also 'one-room mansion' units which are like small studio apartments with a kitchen and a small western-style bathroom. Mansion rents are higher than *apato*. In central Tokyo a decent mansion rental could be 120,000 yen (US$1,000) a month.

Houses are even more expensive to rent. Chances are that you will not be able to find one, and if you do it will probably be so far away from the city centre that commuting will take more than two hours out of your working day.

The Japanese measure their rooms in terms of the *tatami* or the *tsubo*. The *tatami* is their rice straw mat. A *tatami* is 3 feet by 6 feet. The *tsubo* is equal to two *tatamis*. Typical room sizes are 3, 4, 5, 6 and 8 *tatami*. Get a feel for the *tatami* unit size before you start to enquire about housing.

Toilet facilities are generally below western standards. Bathrooms and toilets are usually separate rooms. Older apartments may have Japanese-style squatting toilets, and a shower in the bathroom is

Housing in the suburbs. Note the koi nobori *(climbing carp) on the pole, which represent members of a family – dad, mum and two sons. Carp-shaped kites are flown on 5 May, Boys' Day.*

the exception rather than the rule. If you want to install a shower it would cost you 200,000 yen (US$1,700). Medical people tell us that this is the best way to do your 'dailies', but it is not easy to adjust to.

Apartments are seldom centrally heated and tenants are expected to provide their own heating and air-conditioning equipment. Hot water is not a standard provision, although today most mansions would have individual mansion hot water units.

Finding housing and moving in

If you have decided on the area in which you want to live, go to the local *fudohsanya*, the real estate agent. You can spot his office from the apartment listings in his office window.

If you are more concerned with what you have to pay than where you want to live, you will get all the information you need from the weekly housing information magazine. But it will of course be in Japanese. The ugly head of the language problem raises itself again! In the big cities there are real estate agents who specialise in finding accommodation for expatriates. You will have no language problems with them. Their fee to the tenant is about one month's rent.

The standard deposit when you take over an apartment is one to two months' rent. It is called the *shikikin*. If there has been damage to the property when you move out, the cost of repairs will be deducted from the *shikikin* refunded to you. You have also to pay the landlord a *reikin*, an unrefundable 'gift' or key money, which will be between one and two months' rent. If you add the first month's rent and agent's fee, you may need as much as six months' rent before moving in.

A contract is usually signed between the tenant and the landlord. The normal term of rental lease is two years, but there is usually no penalty for moving out before the expiry of the lease.

Some points on looking for a place to rent

Many Japanese landlords do not want to rent their apartments to foreigners, partly because of the communication problems and partly because they worry about how long the foreign tenant will stay. This limits the number of places available to the foreigner. One way of circumventing this is to have a respectable Japanese guarantor, the *hoshonin*, who will co-sign the tenancy agreement.

It is difficult to find a furnished apartment, and even if the advertisement says 'furnished', it will probably be only partly furnished, or furnished with what you do not want.

We strongly advise you to bring a Japanese friend with you when you inspect apartments up for rent. If you do have a car, check out the parking facilities available. If you do not have a car the proximity of the nearest bus stop or railway station becomes most important. As *apato* and mansions do not have laundry facilities, you should find out how close the nearest coin-laundromat is.

Some landlords are fussy about keeping the apartment clean, or about alterations made by the tenant. There are also landlords who place restrictions on their tenant's lifestyles, such as no pets, no overnight guests or no parties. You must also be aware that landlords have the right to evict tenants if they find out that the apartment is shared with others whose names are not in the agreement.

You may wish to present the landlord with a little gift when you move in, in addition to the *reikin* – such as a bottle of whisky or a can of green tea. The Japanese have a custom of giving a present of dried noodles to their neighbours when they move in and you may wish to follow this custom, too. Noodles symbolise a long-lasting relationship. Landlords have the right to increase the rent every two years when you renew your agreement. The usual rate of increase is 5–10%.

There is one aspect of checking out an apartment that you do not have to worry about in Japan: the safety of the neighbourhood. The crime rate in Japan is the lowest in the world.

Moving out

You have to give your landlord one month's notice in most tenancy agreements if you move out. And it is usually your responsibility to restore the apartment to the condition it was in when you moved in. This includes removing the extras you put in, like a shower. But perhaps these details can be resolved with smiles and a bottle of sake.

Furnishing your apartment

Do not ship out furniture from home. Rooms in Japan are generally too small for furniture used in western countries. Western-style furniture is sold in Japan but you probably will not like the available designs. You should consider antique Japanese furniture, which blends surprisingly well with western decor, as an investment.

There are furniture rental services in most big cities. The classifieds of English periodicals such as the *Weekender* and the *Tokyo Journal* contain advertisements of used furniture offered for sale by expats leaving the country. The Salvation Army sells used furniture at reasonable prices. If you are really desperate keep your eyes open on the days of bulky garbage disposal because often perfectly good household furniture and other items, even television and stereo sets, are put out on the street!

If you want to bring electrical appliances from America, you should consult someone about what will work in Japan. The voltage is 100 volts and the frequency 50 Hz in eastern Japan including Tokyo, but 60 Hz in western Japan. Some appliances, such as pressing irons, toasters, hair-dryers and typewriters will work but at reduced speed and power. Some will not. Personal computers will not.

If the voltage in your country is above 100 volts, you can get transformers or adaptors, but as any electrician will tell you, the frequency is another problem.

Telephones

Telephone services are good but rates are high. To get a phone installed the NTT (Nippon Telegraph and Telephone Corporation) will charge you about 72,000 yen (US$600). You will have to purchase the telephone instrument.

International calls are handled by a private company, KDD (Kokusai Denshin Denwa – International Telecommunication). Direct international dialling is available in all the big cities.

Domestic Help

Many expatriates employ English-speaking maids. Japanese maids are honest, diligent and clean. They can be a great help not only in the house but also in communicating with neighbours and tradesmen. You may have to develop a communication understanding with the maid using sign language and facial expressions.

An experienced maid gets about 250,000–300,000 yen (US$2,100–2,500) a month with room and meals. In addition to these you are also expected to pay her annual bonus of one to three months' pay. Part-time housekeeping maids are paid around 12,500 yen (US$105) a day. Hiring a babysitter is more expensive, as much as 5,500 yen (US$45) an hour. You do not have to give an annual bonus, but you have to provide meals. The Tokyo Domestic Service Centre, telephone (03) 3584-4760, can arrange for a maid, for a fee.

It is important to be aware of the cultural gap when settling the employment details with a maid. You should go through the working conditions carefully, assuming that nothing is the same as at home, to avoid any possible misunderstanding.

Student babysitters are not easily found, but the Tokyo Domestic Service Centre can provide well trained babysitters. Remember that the Japanese babysitter could spoil your child to what you may consider extremes. If this worries you and the babysitter is not trained, you should discuss do's and don'ts with her – that is, if you can get your ideas across and can convince her they are right.

Transportation

In the cities the fastest and cheapest forms of transportation are subways and trains. A private car is expensive to run in Japan and taxis are no faster than trains.

Subways and trains are easier to use than buses because most of them have signs in English. They start at 5:50 a.m. and run to 12:30, after midnight, and hours of service are extended during a special period at the end of April or early May, called the Golden Week. During rush hours trains are very frequent, although they may be terribly crowded. In Tokyo they have 'pushers' packing passengers into trains during the rush hour.

Automatic ticket machines at every station accept both coins and notes, but if the machine does not accept notes look for a change machine, usually located next to the ticket machine. Fares start from around 160 yen (about US$1.35). If you do not know how much you have to pay get a ticket for the minimum fare. When you get out of your destination station a man or a machine checks your ticket and you have to top up the fare. You have to hold on to your ticket because of the check at the exits, even if you have got the right fare. If you have lost your ticket or use an old ticket you will be charged the maximum fare.

The subway lines and route map is normally adjacent to the ticket machine which also shows the fares to the different stations. At the major stations in the cities or at information centres maps in English are available.

Riding the buses is equally easy and very convenient for short distances. You can also see where you are going and if you know the area you can see if you have taken the wrong bus, or the right bus in the wrong direction. In some cities you board the bus at the back and in some cities in the front. There is a ticket and change machine in the bus. In urban areas it is usually a flat rate, 210 yen (about US$1.75). In rural areas you get on the bus at the back and get a ticket without paying. You pay according to distance travelled when you get off in the front of the bus. You have to signal the driver with the stop button, which is usually near the seat. Rural buses do not have change machines, so you should have small change.

Books of tickets are sold for both buses and trains. They are cheaper than single journey tickets. Savings can be made by buying season passes valid for 1, 3 or 6 months. Alternatively, buy a *kaisuken* or series of 11 tickets (you pay for 10 and get 1 free) between two known destinations for trips along regular routes. One-day tickets for multiple trips are also available.

Taxi-drivers in Japan are honest and efficient and take pride in their work. But very few speak recognisable English. They are not reckless and do not drive with mad *kamikaze* abandon as some guide books suggest. They are easily picked up in the large cities. To hail a taxi hold your hand out with your fingers pointing downwards. A red light on the windscreen means the taxi is free. A green light means it is occupied. The colour system doesn't seem logical, but you will get used to it. A yellow light means it is on call.

All taxi passenger doors are controlled by the driver. The mechanism not only unlocks the door but also swings it open. So stand away from the door when the taxi pulls up in front of you.

One of the frustrations of a *gaijin* hailing a taxi is that many drivers do not like to pick up foreigners because they are afraid of language problems. Do not be upset if a taxi ignores your frantic waving. It is not a racial bias, just a communication hang-up the taxi-drivers have.

All taxis have meters. The flag-drop or initial charge is 650 yen (about US$5.50). They do not expect tips. There is a late night surcharge of 20%. In the entertainment areas it is very difficult to find an empty taxi late at night.

There a method of getting a taxi after midnight in the Roppongi and Shinjuku districts that I cannot vouch for, but it is worth telling in case it is true. If you stick out your hand with two fingers up like the V-for-victory sign the taxi-driver will read it as a signal that you are willing to pay twice the total on the meter. Three fingers for three times. Do not wave for a taxi with two hands and all ten digits outstretched.

Unless you speak Japanese well, you should get someone to write out the address of your destination before you get into the taxi. This

The Shinkansen super-express.

applies even if you want to go to a well known place like the Mitsubishi Corporation building, because the way you say it is not the way the taxi-driver says it. If it is not on a well known street you should get it marked on a map or a sketch, with some additional information like giving a nearby landmark for the taxi driver. Not all streets in Japan have names! This is particularly important in Tokyo.

In spite of all their slick systems in technology and management, the postal address system of Tokyo is one unimaginable nightmare. It is as though they can't face the horrific task of re-numbering the buildings in Tokyo and its outskirts. The city has grown too fast. Never look for a place walking down the street reading numbers and working out the logic of the numbering sequence. Ask someone. We have a suspicion that the wonderful Japanese proverb, 'Ask once and be embarrassed once. Do not ask and you will be embarrassed all your life' might have something to do with the Tokyo building numbers system!

For long distance travel there are efficient express and local trains.

The *Shinkansen*, commonly known as the 'bullet train', connects the major cities of Japan. The stops are announced in English. One can buy a ticket on these trains in advance and we advise you to do so if you intend to travel on a weekend or during a holiday period. Note that there are very few smoking carriages on these fast trains. And, of course, there is the airway network to fly you from city to city.

An absolutely English friend of ours had a delightful experience on the bullet train that hit him and his very proper wife with severe culture shock. It illustrates one aspect of the Japanese.

A middle-aged Japanese, quite obviously a businessman, in his beautifully cut pin-striped suit, sat opposite them, very sedate and frowning with the problems he had brought from the office. As the train went on his frown disappeared and he stood up and took his large briefcase down from the rack. He took a bottle of whisky out of it. He even had a glass. He proceeded to sip whisky with much smacking of lips in apparent relish. It pleased our friend, who had some Scots blood in him, and his wife to see that the man was not all *homo economicus*. But the frequency of his sips started increasing. The lip-smacking and the *Ahh*'s grew louder and increasingly appreciative.

His face flushed slowly. He took off his coat. There were more *ahh*'s and our English friends thought they saw his face settle down to a fixed smile of content. He took off his tie. His hand appeared to be less steady and the shots he poured seemed to get larger. He unbuttoned his shirt. There was by now a grin of happiness. He loosened his belt. (He had taken off his shoes much earlier, when the bottle was a quarter down.)

They watched the level in the bottle. It passed the halfway mark. Then he stood up. To their utter English embarrassment he took off his trousers and placed them neatly on the seat beside him. He had quite decent baggy underwear. He brought the briefcase down again. He took a light *kimono* out of it and proceeded at once to divest himself of shirt and vest, completely unaware of the open-mouthed stares of the *gaijin* and his pretty woman, and put on his *yukata*. The *ahh*'s of appreciation were now being gasped with an enthusiasm that would have gladdened the heart of the hardest of Scottish distillers.

Then he started to sing. Softly. It sounded like nice old sentimental tunes to them. The subdued singing appeared to dry his throat because he found it necessary to wet it with whisky very, very frequently.

Our English friend suddenly squeezed his wife's hand. She started up and looked across at their dignified travelling companion. He was pouring out the last tot, holding the bottle above the glass and shaking it. They watched the bottle die. He gulped it down, drew his legs up under him, curled up on the seat, and fell asleep instantly.

> "The natives are famed for their diligence in the work place. Are you prepared to work as long, and as hard, to satisfy their demanding standards?"
>
> —*SWET Newsletter*, November 1988

Driving in Japan

Your international driving licence is valid for one year. You have to apply for a Japanese driving licence at a driver's licence test centre. Bring your licence and its official Japanese translation from the Japan Automobile Federation or your embassy, Alien Registration Certificate, passport and a 2.4 x 3 cm photo. You will be given an eye test at the office. The licence fee is 3,900 yen (about US$33). The expiry date of Japanese driving licences depends on your age, hence your birthday is the cut-off day. Licences are given for three years. An eye test is part of the process of renewing a driving licence.

If you do not have a driving licence you must take two written tests, in English, and two driving tests. You have to learn from an approved driving school. A driving course costs you around 350,000–400,000 yen (US$2,940–3,360).

The international traffic sign system has been adopted in Japan. These are the signs one sees in Europe and they are different from traffic signs in the USA. They drive on the left in Japan, as one does in the UK. Speed limits are 30 kph in the cities, 40 kph on rural roads, 60 kph on highways and 100 kph on expressways. The major problem for foreigners is that there are very few signs in English. Don't assume that this is not a problem from the English signs you see in the cities.

The alcohol limit for drunken driving is strict. You will be considered alcohol-influenced if found with 0.25 milligrams of alcohol or more per litre of breath or per millilitre of blood, regardless of external appearance. Refusal to take a breath test can result in a fine of 30,000 yen (US$250). The maximum penalty for drunken driving is the revocation of your driving licence. To get it back you must go to re-education sessions and do community service.

The other problem, as one might expect in a country with limited flat land, is parking. The metered parking rate is 300 yen (US$2.50) an hour. It is 300–600 yen (US$2.50–5.00) an hour at car parks but large supermarkets and department stores have their own carparks and will reimburse you for parking for purchases over a certain total.

The Japan Automobile Federation, at 3-5-8 Shibakoen, Minato-ku, Tokyo 105-0011, tel: (03) 3436-2811, fax: (03) 3436-3009, publishes the best booklet on traffic laws, *Driver's Map of Japan*.

Car rental is expensive, about 4,500 yen (US$38) for 6 hours, or from about 6,800 yen (US$57) for 24 hours. With the frequent traffic jams in the cities, it is not recommended. We also do not recommend bringing a car into Japan. It's like bringing coals to Newcastle. Remember that the cost of distribution and retailing in Japan is very high compared to other countries. Spares will be very costly.

Car owners pay road taxes and insurance, *shaken*. Cars are inspected every three years, and every year after they are ten years old. The inspection fee is 10,000 yen (US$85) but costs soar because inspectors usually find something wrong that needs to be fixed. Private cars must have maintenance checks, *tenken*, every six months.

Parking is a major consideration if you plan to own a car. To obtain registration and licence plates, you must show you have an off-street parking space for your car, certified by your local police station. There is no all-night street parking allowed. Parking space rental a month is from 10,000 to 30,000 yen upwards (US$85–250).

Shopping

Although Japan produces the finest quality consumer goods at low costs, prices in the shops in Japan will astonish you. The same camera or radio that you bought at home will be much more expensive. This is mainly because the costs of distribution and retailing are very high. Once you have got over this shock, you will find shopping in Japan exciting because of the variety, and the interesting things which you have never seen at home.

The department stores will most probably have anything you need. There are English-speaking staff, or sometimes a Foreign Customers' Liaison Office, at most big stores like Seibu, Matsuya, Takashimaya and Isetan in Tokyo.

The shopping areas in Tokyo are Ginza for the top quality (though now thought to be the shopping place for the older generation), and Shinjuku and Shibuya, where more young people shop. For trendy clothes look for the boutiques in Harajuku and Aoyama. Akihabara is the place for electronic goods, Asakusa for traditional Japanese items, Ueno for the open discount market, and Tsukiji for Japanese food.

Then there are the specialist stores and stores that have a special character. Tokyu Hands is one of them. It is not just a do-it-yourself person's store. It has gifts, household items, party things and almost anything you can think of. The Marui department store is another. Stores offer instalment payment plans and issue their own credit cards with credit limits varying from store to store. There are also tax-free shops selling cameras, electronic goods, etc. You pay for the goods there and collect them at the airport. The system is quite reliable.

Prices are generally fixed in Japan, although at some discount stores you can bargain the price down. A consumption tax of 5% is added; for some products it is included in the price. There are, in addition, local or municipal taxes applied to lodging and meals, ranging from 3% to 10%, depending on the total amount of the bill. Tipping is not the standard practice, but many restaurants add a 10% service charge to the bill. Terms are usually cash, but credit

Ginza Avenue, looking north from the Ginza crossing.

cards can be used in most big stores. Personal cheques are not accepted, except at some supermarkets serving a foreign clientele.

Stores in Japan generally provide excellent service. Staff are well-trained and courteous. They will have the answers to your questions about the goods, but there may be a language problem. Large items will be delivered to your house and they will accept returns provided you have the receipt and a plausible reason for returning the items.

Shopping hours are generally 10 a.m. to 6 p.m. Most stores are closed on Sundays and public holidays. Even the few that open on Sundays would most probably be closed for New Year festivities (1–3 January) and for the mid-August *obon* festival. Supermarkets are usually open from 9 a.m. to 7 p.m. all year round, and there are some convenience stores which may even stay open during the New Year holiday period.

There are supermarkets in residential areas, and in Tokyo a few supermarkets, such as the National Azabu Supermarket, Kinokuniya and Meidiya, cater to expatriates. Their prices are higher than those in ordinary Japanese supermarkets as they do not get the same turnover, but they stock most of the things that you bought at home and they all provide a home delivery service.

Clustered near the train stations are the *shotengai*, shopping streets. Here you will find convenience stores like 7-Eleven, smaller than the supermarkets but open 24 hours, 'mom-and-pop' stores, and a variety of other kinds of shops. The *shotengai* become very crowded in the late afternoon every day by housewives shopping for dinner. The Japanese prefer to buy their food daily and have it fresh rather than do all their shopping on the weekend.

Education

Education for your children in Japan is not a major problem if you are going to stay in one of the major cities. There are many good schools for foreigners. Your children will not only get the same education as they would get in your country but also be exposed to Japanese culture and to children of other nationalities.

In Japan there are 24 schools offering education in English; 14 of these are in the Tokyo-Yokohama area. There are international schools in Kobe, Kyoto, Hiroshima, Sapporo, Fukuoka and Okinawa. Tokyo also has French, German, Indonesian, Korean and Chinese schools. These are all private schools and costs are very high. They maintain high academic standards and one survey reports that standard test scores are well above US national norms. Facilities and staff are generally very good.

International schools do not follow the Japanese academic year of April to March, but the US-European year of September to mid-June. School hours are usually from 8:15 a.m. to about 4 p.m. through five days a week. Some schools are affiliated with church organisations, but such schools generally keep their religious affiliations in the background and do not limit intake to students of their religion.

There are waiting lists for most international schools. You should apply as early as you can. Don't forget to get documents and references from your children's school before you leave for Japan.

Foreign students can attend Japanese public schools and universities if they have a competency in Japanese appropriate to the education level. Foreign students will, however, have to sit for the university entrance examinations and compete with the local students for a place in the university. There are a few universities geared towards foreigners, with English as the medium of instruction, such as Sophia University and the International Christian University.

Information on international schools is given in Chapter 9. The Association of International Education, Japan, at 4-5-29, Komaba, Meguro-ku, Tokyo 153, tel: (03) 5454-5577, 5211, gives you information on entry into universities. For high school students who have been studying in Japan and want to go to US universities, the Japan-United States Educational Commission (Fulbright Program) has all the information. They can be reached at Sanno Grand Building, 206, 2-14-2 Nagata-cho, Chiyoda-ku, Tokyo 100-0014, tel: (03) 3580-3235, fax: (03) 3580-1217, email fulcomj@juscc.go.jp.

There are a great many organisations providing Japanese language and Japanese arts and crafts lessons for adult foreigners. Courses are advertised in English newspapers and periodicals such as the *Japan Times*, *Tokyo Journal* and *Weekender*.

Medical Care

The standard of medicine and medical care in Japan is one of the highest in the world. But there are major differences. Japanese medical practice tends to be far more specialised than in the West, and, as in industry, they approach a medical problem with teamwork. You must be prepared for a different style of professionalism if you go to Japanese doctors. On one hand the general practitioner may appear cold and too scientific to you, but on the other hand I know of a case where the doctors did everything possible to keep the wife of a surgical patient informed and even allowed her to watch the operation on closed circuit television.

In the big cities many doctors speak English and have been trained overseas. There are also hospitals organised for English-speaking patients; some are listed in Chapter 9. The Tokyo English Life Line (TELL) gives you information on medical services, including mental health: telephone (03) 3960-4099, counselling services (03) 3960-4084, 4004, email tellnet@majic.co.jp.

The British embassy in Tokyo has a yellow bilingual medical data card designed for accidents and emergencies. We suggest you get one, fill it out and keep it on your person all the time.

Some Medical Words

Accident – *Jiko*
Ambulance – *Kyukyusha*
Appointment – *Yoyaku*
Consultation – *Shinsatsu*
Doctor – *Isha*
Examination/test – *Kensa*
Hospital – *Byoin*
Hospitalisation – *Nyuin*
Injury – *Kega*
Medicine/drug – *Kusuri*
Painful – *Itai*
Treatment – *Chiryo*

In an emergency dial 119, the Fire Department, which operates the ambulance service. Many Japanese hospitals are reluctant to admit foreigners for fear of language problems. If you don't know whether or not a hospital will admit a foreign patient, send the ambulance to one of the English-speaking hospitals listed in Chapter 9.

Get yourself covered by the National Health Insurance scheme, even if your medical insurance from home covers you for treatment in Japan. Being registered with the National Health Insurance, *Kokumin Kenko Hoken*, gives you easier access to doctors and hospitals. Most

Japanese health services are provided through this scheme, which is open to foreigners.

Apply at the welfare bureau (*Kokumin Kenko Hokenka*, National Health Insurance Section) of your local town or ward office (*ku-* or *shi-yakusho*). You will be given a card, *Kenko Hokensho*, to present at hospitals and clinics. The National Health Insurance does not cover pregnancy and childbirth.

The alternative is to get one of the medical insurance schemes offered by private companies.

There are the usual private doctors, clinics and private hospitals. Almost all hospitals have an outpatient department which you can go to directly without a referral from a doctor. On your first visit you must bring with you your medical insurance card, *Kenko Hokensho*. They will give you a registration card for subsequent visits. But if there has been a gap of a few months between your visits to the hospital you may need the *Kenko Hokensho* again. You will not be denied treatment if you do not have the *Kenko Hokensho*, but the cost will be much higher. Medicine is prescribed and given out at the hospital or the doctor's clinic, and not at drugstores.

If hospitalisation is required, a referral will be made by a private doctor to the hospital with which he has connections. Your doctor will not be allowed to treat you in the hospital unless it is an exceptional case. In general, whether you are allocated a private room or put in a ward with many beds depends not so much on whether you are willing to pay but on your treatment needs. Private rooms cost a lot more.

Patients are asked to bring their own clothing, towels, eating utensils and sometimes even bedding. Family members are expected to help with the patients' personal needs. One does not hand over the patient to the hospital and leave everything to the nurses as one does in the West.

English-speaking nurses are rare. Japanese food is served but most hospitals will allow a foreigner to eat food brought in by the family. You have to ask.

If you are coming to stay in Japan it is very important that you bring your medical records with you. Remember the ubiquitous language problem. And if you are on special medication, you should bring an adequate initial stock for use until you find out how you can get supplies in Japan. There are special drugstores which may have what you need. Some hotels have drugstores selling foreign drugs. These will cost a lot more than in your country. Vitamins in particular are very expensive in Japan.

In addition to western medicine, there are many doctors practising oriental medicine, such as acupuncture (*hari*), acupressure (*shiatsu*) and herbal medicine. These holistic health and medical systems include excellent preventive measures and are often used in combination with western medical treatment. The oriental medicine doctors have gone through many years of rigorous compulsory training to get their qualifications. English-speaking practitioners of oriental medicine are rare but there are some listed in English language publications. The National Health Insurance does not cover their services.

Public Safety

Japan is one of the safest countries in the world. The crime rate is very low and one can walk anywhere alone after dark in Japan. This low level of crime is partly because of the attitude of the people and partly due to the large police force. You will see the little police posts, *koban*, everywhere. Their system is to spread out the police posts in small units, from which the policemen patrol the streets on bicycles, rather than operate large police stations. It keeps the police in close touch with the people. Policemen are armed.

But do not let the peacefulness make you complacent. The pickpockets, bag and wallet snatchers, burglars and occasional drunken molesters are still around even in Japan. The recent highlight on the problem of sexual harassment has led to a new term being coined, *seku hara*, i.e., sexual harassment.

— Chapter Four —

COMMUNICATING WITH THE JAPANESE

If you have never left your country and have had very little exposure to foreigners, your sense of isolation and insecurity when people around you are talking in a strange language is something you will have to get used to. In shops, trains and restaurants you could get the feeling of being rejected and alone in a crowd. If you let it worry you, you will start thinking that they are talking about you all the time. So learn to ignore the unintelligible chatter around you. Or take advantage of your constant exposure to Japanese and learn the language.

Japanese is not an easy language to learn, mainly because of the different styles you have to use depending on who you are talking to, and because you will have to learn a different script. But do not worry too much about the writing. Memorising the characters will be easier than you imagine.

Like all people, the Japanese will be amused and delighted to hear the *gaijin* saying something in their language. But when you start to get fluent you will meet the opposite reaction with strangers. Somehow they feel it is an intrusion into their privacy when they unexpectedly meet a *gaijin* who speaks fluently. In fact they really do not know how to react.

Learning Japanese, however, requires a substantial investment in both time and money. A great deal of effort must be put in just to determine if you have the interest and stamina to learn Japanese. Learning to use the socially proper phrases is one aspect of spoken Japanese that will take years, and which will no doubt result in some embarrassment.

The Language, Nippon-go

Pronunciation presents no problems. There are only a few new sounds to an English speaker, like the French *r* and the German *g*, which an English speaker learning French or German has to master. There are no tones as in Chinese. Every syllable in a word is given equal treatment; there are no marked accents on particular syllables.

As in English, there are five vowels:

a as in *car*, *far*

i as in *week*, *beet* but shorter, as in *bit*

u as in *two*, but shorter; or as in *put* with the lips not rounded but left slack

e as in *bed*, or the *a* in *hay*

o as in *on*, *cot*, with the lips slightly more rounded.

There are variations of these five vowel sounds: a-, i-, u-, e-, o-. They are pronounced in the same way but longer. They are written with a *u* after the usual character. Thus the longer *to* sound is written with two characters – *to* and *u*; *tou*.

The basic sounds are combined to give sounds like *kyo* (keeoh), *jya* (jar), *sha* (shah), etc. *Kya*, for example, is written with the *ki* character and a smaller *ya* character following it. Most of the consonants are pronounced as in English but in a softer way.

Two new sounds you will have to learn are the *n* which is sounded through the nose, and *tsu*. *Tsu* is the same sound as the Chinese *tsu*; something like the *ts* in cats; almost a *z* sound. Where sounds are coalesced, as in *Nikko*, for example, a smaller *tsu* character is used, in this case between the *ni* character and the *ko* character. It indicates that the pronunciation has to be *Nik-ko*, and not the gentler *Ni-ko*.

There are clear grammatical rules with no exceptions and no irregular verbs. The subject is always followed by *wa* and the object by *o*. The verb is placed at the end of a sentence and adjectives precede the noun which they modify. There are no genders. Verbs are conjugated as in European languages.

Written Japanese consists of two sets of phonetic alphabets, both with the same 46 sounds but written in a different way; rather like the English ordinary script and italics. These are the *hiragana* and *katakana*. *Hiragana* is a rounded, curly script. *Katakana* is mainly straight lines and more angular. *Katakana* is used for foreign words.

In addition to *hiragana* and *katakana*, the Japanese use Chinese characters. These are ideograms derived originally from pictures. They call these *Kanji*.The problem with *kanji* is that one has to learn the two or three different pronunciations for each character. There is no indication of the pronunciation in the *kanji* character. Two thousand *kanji* characters are taught in school but the more highbrow novelists use more *kanji* than these two thousand. The pronunciation is often written in small *hiragana* beside unusual *kanji*. And there are many surnames with *kanji* that are not in the basic two thousand.

Traditional Japanese is written in vertical columns and one reads from right to left. Their books thus open the other way. But today a lot of writing is done in horizontal rows, reading from left to right as in English.

Japanese is a fairly regular language as opposed to a language full of idioms like English, Chinese or Malay. There are very few variations across the country. The greatest variation across Japan is in the pronunciation.

Knowing Japanese will be a huge asset to anyone living in Japan. But in the large cities you can get by with English and a few common phrases of greeting, gratitude, requests and simpler questions. A list of such phrases is given here. The words in parentheses are optional; they make the expression more polite. Some of these phrases do not have an exact equivalent in English and the translations given here do not carry the full nuances.

Greetings, Thanks, Apologies and Other Common Phrases

Ohayo gozaimasu – Good morning
Konnichiwa – Good afternoon
Konbanwa – Good evening
Oyasuminasai – Goodnight
Sayonara – Goodbye (used only when one is not going to see the other person for some time)
Shitsurei shimasu – Goodbye (although used for partings as 'goodbye', it is, literally, *I have been rude*. Used on the phone when ringing off and as *Excuse me*)
Ja mata – See you! (casual)

Hai – Yes
Ie – No (but used very, very seldom)
Hajimemashite – How do you do? (at first meeting only)
Ogenki desuka? – How are you?
Hai, genki desu – I am fine
(*Domo*) *Arigato gozaimasu* – Thank you (very much)
Do itashimashite – You're welcome (in reply to *Thank you*)
Ie, Kekko desu – No thank you

(*Domo*) *Sumimasen* – I'm (very) sorry, or excuse me

Dozo – Please (go ahead, help yourself)

Yoroshiku onegai-shimasu – Please (when asking assistance or for a favour). Also, *I'm pleased to meet you, I trust you will guide me well, Let's do our best*

Osewani narimashita – Thank you for your kindness (for something already done), literally, *I have become indebted to you*

Itadakimasu – I receive this food/drink gratefully (said like *bon appétit* before eating or drinking)

Gochisosama deshita – Thank you for a delicious meal (said after eating or drinking)

Itte kimasu – I'm leaving (when leaving home or the office on business)

Itte rasshiai – Safe return! (in response to *Itte kimasu*)

Tadaima – I'm back

Okaeri nasai – Welcome back

Expressions of Empathy

The following expressions are commonly used in addition to the above greetings to maintain smooth human relationships.

Otsukaresama (*deshita*) – Thank you for your hard work. We have worked hard, haven't we? (Farewell phrase used at the end of the day or on completion of some joint work. Literally, *You must be tired.*)

Gokurosama deshita – Thank you for your hard work (used by superiors to subordinates)

Taihen desu ne – It's hard work, isn't it? Terrible, isn't it?

Ganbatte kudasai – Good luck! Keep up the good work! Please do your best.

Ganbarimasho – Let's try our best

Kio tsukete (*kudasai*) – (Please) take care (farewell expression)

Daijobu desuka? – Is it all right? Are you all right?

Odaijini – Take care of yourself (to someone who is ill)
Atsui desune – It's hot, isn't it?
Samui desune – It's cold, isn't it?
Oishii desune – Delicious, isn't it?
Oisogashii tokoro (*sumimasen*) – Excuse me for bothering you when you are so busy
So desune? – Yes, isn't it? Isn't it so? Well, let me see ...

Other Useful Expressions

Sumisu to iimasu – My name is Smith
Amerikajin desu – I am American
Shigoto de kimashita – I came here to work, or on business
Nihon wa hajimete desu – This is my first time in Japan
Onamae wa? – What is your name?
Tanaka-san desuka? – Mr/Mrs/Miss Tanaka?
Eigo wakarimasuka – Do you speak English?
Nihongo wa wakarimasen – I do not understand Japanese
Sukoshi wakarimasu – I understand a little bit
Ote-arai wa doko desuka? – Where is the washroom?
Denwa wa arimasuka – Is there a telephone here?
Heya wa arimasuka? – Do you have a room?
Moshi-moshi – Hello (on the phone only)
Tanaka-san wo onegaishimasu – May I speak to Mr/Mrs/Miss Tanaka?
Chotto matte kudasai – Just a moment, please
Mata atode kakemasu – I'll call back later
Kore wa nan desuka – What is this?
So desuka? – Is that so?
(*Totemo*) *suki desu* – I like it (very much)
Amari sukija nai desu – I don't like that very much
Aishite imasu – I love you

Shopping

Ningyo/enpitsu arimasuka? – Do you have dolls/pencils?
Motto ooki no arimasuka – Have you got a larger one/size?
Hoka no iro arimasuka? – Have you got another colour?
Kore wa ikura desuka? – How much is this?
Takai desune – Expensive, isn't it?
Motto yasui no wa arimasuka? – Have you got a cheaper one?
Kore kudasai – I'll take this

At a Restaurant

Menyu o kudasai – A menu, please
Biiru o kudasai – A beer, please
Biiru o moh ippon kudasai – Another bottle of beer, please
Omizu/ocha kudasai – Water/green tea, please
Kohhii to kohcha kudasai – Coffee and tea, please
Osake arimasuka? – Do you have *sake*? (Note that the *o* before *sake* is an honorific or polite prefix)
Oishii desu – It's delicious
Okanjo onegaishimasu – The check, please
Gochisosama – That was delicious, thank you

In a Taxi

Ginza made onegaishimasu – To the Ginza, please
Massugu itte kudasai – Straight on, please
Tsugi no kado o migi desu – Right at the next corner
Tsugi no shingo o hidari desu – Left at the next signals
Koko de iidesu – Please stop here
Sumimasen ga mattete kudasai – Will you please wait for me

In Emergencies

Tasukete (kudasai) – (Please) help me
Kyukyusha onegaishimasu – An ambulance, please
Patoroh-ru-kar onegaishimasu – Send a patrol car, please

Kaji desu – There is a fire
Jiko desu – It is an accident
Dorobo desu – There was a burglary
Jusho wa … – The address is …
Shukketsu shite imasu – He/she is bleeding
Ishiki ga arimasen – He/she is unconscious
Yakedo o shimashita – He/she got burned
Kossetsu desu – He/she has broken a bone
Shinzo hossa desu – It is a heart attack
Shikyu onegaishimasu – Please hurry up
Itai desu – It hurts
Ninshin shite imasu – She is pregnant
Penicirrin ni arerugi ga arimasu – I am allergic to penicillin

Reading Maps and Asking Directions

ken – prefecture
gun – ward
shi, or *to* (Tokyo only) – city
machi – town or quarter in a city
ku – ward (inside Tokyo only)
mura – village
dori – avenue
cho – street
chome – block
ban – number
biru – building (but note that this sounds like *biiru* – beer!)

san, or *yama* – mountain
ji, or *otera* – temple
jo, or *shiro* – castle
shima, or *to*, or *jima* – island
sawa, or *zawa* – swamp
kawa, or *gawa* – river

wan – bay
tohge – mountain pass
mine – peak
oka – hill
saki – cape
han-to – peninsula (literally, half-island)

USEFUL VOCABULARY

Numerals

The Japanese use two sets of words for numbers. One, the *ichi-ni-san-shi* series, is derived from the Chinese and the other, the *hitotsu-futatsu-mittsu* series, they developed themselves. The *hitotsu-futatsu-mittsu* series is used for counting things. If the number of your house was 123, you would say *ichi-ni-san*. You would ask for *futatsu* – '*Futatsu kudasai*' – if you were buying two pieces.

They also use classifiers like a 'stick' of celery, and these classifier words can mask the sound of the numeral part of the word. For example, *ippon* is one bottle, abbreviated from *ichi-pon*. To speak good Japanese one has to use the correct classifier, but you don't have to worry too much about getting it right in everyday communication. For counting people they have another series.

The numbers		For counting	For people
1	*Ichi*	*Hitotsu*	*Hitori*
2	*Ni*	*Futatsu*	*Futari*
3	*San*	*Mittsu*	*San-nin*
4	*Shi*	*Yottsu*	*Yonin*
5	*Go*	*Itsutsu*	*Gonin*
6	*Roku*	*Muttsu*	*Rokunin*
7	*Shichi*	*Nanatsu*	*Shichinin*
8	*Hachi*	*Yattsu*	*Hachinin*
9	*Kyu*	*Kokonotsu*	*Kunin*
10	*Ju*	*Jukko/Jutoh*	*Junin*

Be careful about enunciating *mittsu* and *muttsu* clearly. You could get six when you only wanted three!

The hours are dealt with by adding *ji* after the number. Thus *san-ji* is three o'clock.

11 *Ju-ichi*
12 *Ju-ni*
13 *Ju-san*
14 *Ju-shi*

20 *Ni-ju*
21 *Niju-ichi*

30 *Sanju*
40 *Yon-ju*

100 *Hyaku*
101 *Hyaku-ichi*
111 *Hyaku-ju-ichi*

300 *Sanbyaku*
700 *Nanahyaku* (Note that the other series word is used for 700)
800 *Happyaku*
1,000 *Sen*

The Japanese use a unit of ten thousand, *man*, for the larger figures. This takes some getting used to: the mental adjustment is not easy. 20,000 is *ni-man*. 100,000 is *ju-man*. One million is *hyaku-man*.

There is also a unit for a hundred million, *oku*. Two hundred million is *ni-oku*.

Calendar

Sunday *Nichiyobi* (day of the sun)

Monday	*Getsuyobi* (moon day)
Tuesday	*Kayobi* (fire day)
Wednesday	*Suiyobi* (water day)
Thursday	*Mokuyobi* (wood day)
Friday	*Kinyobi* (gold day)
Saturday	*Doyobi* (earth day)

From Monday …	*Getsuyobi kara …*
… until Friday	*… Kinyobi made*

Today	*Kyo*
Yesterday	*Kinoh*
Tomorrow	*Ashita*
One day	*Ichi-nichi*
Two days	*Futsuka*
Three days	*Mikka*
Since three days ago	*Mikka mae kara*
For two days	*Futsuka kan*

This week	*Konshu*
Last week	*Senshu*
Next week	*Raishu*
One week	*Isshu*
Two weeks	*Nishukan*

The months are known by number.

January	*Ichigatsu*
February	*Nigatsu*
March	*Sangatsu*
April	*Shigatsu*
May	*Gogatsu*
June	*Rokugatsu*
July	*Shichigatsu*

August	*Hachigatsu*
September	*Kugatsu*
October	*Jugatsu*
November	*Juichigatsu*
December	*Junigatsu*
This month	*Kongetsu* (note that it is *getsu*, not *gatsu* as in the month names)
Last month	*Sengetsu*
Next month	*Raigetsu*
Next month	*Ikkagetsu* (*ka* is the classifier for counting months)
Two months	*Nikagetsu*
Three months	*Sankagetsu*
Four months	*Yonkagetsu kan*

Transportation

Train	*Densha* (literally, electric train)
Subway	*Chikatetsu*
Bus	*Basu*
Taxi	*Takushi*
Car	*Kuruma*
Motorcycle	*Ohtobai*
Bicycle	*Jitensha*
Station	*Eki*
Ticket	*Kippu*
Local train	*Futsu*
Express train	*Kyuko*
Transfer	*Norikae*
Bus stop	*Teiryujo*
Pass	*Teiki*
Coupon tickets	*Menkyosho*
Driver (chauffeur)	*Untenshu-san*

Parking lot	*Chushajo*
Expressway	*Kosoku*
Gas station	*Gasorin sutando*
Airport	*Kukoh*
Luggage	*Nimotsu*
Entrance	*Iriguchi*
Exit	*Deguchi*
North	*Kita*
South	*Minami*
East	*Higashi*
West	*Nishi*

Around Town

Department store	*Depato*
Supermarket	*Supa*
24-hour store	*Konbinensu sutoa*
Bank	*Ginko*
Post office	*Yubinkyoku*
Ward office	*Kuyakusho*
City office	*Shiyakusho*
Tax office	*Zeimusho*
Immigration office	*Nyukoku Kanri Kyoku*
Embassy	*Taishikan*
Consulate	*Ryojikan*
School	*Gakko*
Drugstore	*Kusuriya*
Greengrocer	*Yaoya*
Butcher	*Nikuya*
Fishmonger	*Sakanaya*
Bakery	*Panya*
Bookstore	*Honya*

Stationery shop	*Bunbohguya*
Electrical appliance shop	*Denkiya*
Beauty salon	*Biyoh-in* (Be careful about this one; *byoin* means hospital)
Barber	*Tokoya*
Restaurant	*Resutoran*
Coffee shop	*Kissaten*
Movie theatre	*Eigakan*
Park	*Koen*
Amusement park	*Yuenchi*
Temple	*Otera*
Shrine	*Jinjya*
Church	*Kyokai*

Foreign Names and Words

The Japanese have taken in many foreign words into their language but you may not recognise them when a Japanese uses them. Because of the limitations of their phonetic system they have had to modify them. They also have a tendency to abbreviate words they adopt.

California	*Kariforunia*
Los Angeles	*Rosu Anzeresu*, or *Rosu*
England	*Igirisu*
Germany	*Doitsu*
Berlin	*Berurin*
Hamburg	*Hamburugu*
Switzerland	*Suisu*
Zurich	*Churihhi*
David	*Debbido*
Pierre	*Pieru*
Carol	*Kyaroru*
Katherine	*Kyasarin*
Clark	*Kuraku*

Smith	*Sumisu*
McDonald	*Makudonarudo*

You can have fun trying to translate different western names into the Japanese version. We knew a couple who had the unusual Cornish name of Tregaskis. Before they went to Japan on a holiday we sat around working out different Japanese versions of Tregaskis. But he decided that it would be too optimistic to expect the Japanese to say Tregaskis. So they checked into the hotel as Mr and Mrs Smith, Sumisu.

One day, Mrs Tregaskis had to show her passport to the cashier in the hotel when she was cashing a large sum in traveller's cheques. As the cashier returned her passport he said with a little smile, in perfect English, "Ahh … You're travelling with Mr Smith, Mrs Tregaskis?"

Food/Drink

Coffee	*Kohhii*
Milk	*Miruku*
Coke	*Kohra*
Orange juice	*Orenji jusu*
Beer	*Biiru* (*Biru* is building)
Soup	*Supu*
Hors d'oeuvres	*Odoburu*
Sandwich	*Sando-ichi*
Bread	*Pan* (from the Portuguese)
Hamburger	*Hanbahgah*
French fries	*Furaido poteto*
Steak	*Suteki*
Salad	*Sarada*
Rice and curry	*Kare raisu*
Dessert	*Dezato*
Ice-cream	*Aisukurimu*

(More food words are listed in Chapter 7.)

Shopping

Television	*Terebi*
Radio	*Rajio*
Radio-cassette	*Rajikase*
Video	*Bideo*
Record	*Rekodo*
Personal computer	*Pasokon*
Word processor	*Wapuro*
Air-conditioner	*Eakon*
Pressing iron	*Airon*
Hair-dryer	*Doraiyah*
Dress	*Doresu* (long dress)
	Wanpisu (shorter dress)
Skirt	*Sukarto*
Pantyhose	*Pansuto*
Shirt	*Shatsu*
Socks	*Sokkusu*
Table	*Tehburu*
Cigarettes	*Tabako*

How to Learn Japanese

That is, if you want to learn Japanese.

The best and quickest way is to go to a Japanese language school or to get a private tutor. You can get a tutor to come to your house or office for 3,000–5,000 yen (US$25–42) per hour. Make sure that the tutor has a teaching licence from a language institute and has taken courses on teaching Japanese to foreigners. Check what experience he or she has had. Recommendations are not always reliable. You could reduce the cost of private lessons by getting a group of people to learn Japanese together.

Schools vary a great deal, from the intensive crash courses to slow and easy sessions paced for housewives who are in no hurry to master the language. The address of a Japanese language school in the metropolitan area is given in Chapter 9. Language schools usually offer group and private lessons. They are advertised in the classifieds of the *Tokyo Journal* and the *Japan Times*. The classifieds also list contacts for the cheaper, but more doubtful way of learning Japanese: the 'language exchange' system. You teach your language to a Japanese and get Japanese lessons in return.

A good start is to get a language tape series like the *Linguaphone* series. It will give you an idea of the problems involved in learning the language, and help you to decide whether or not you want to embark on the major project of mastering Japanese. It is a long haul, but a fascinating and rewarding one.

One tip if you are learning the language; stick labels or put cards on everything in the house with its Japanese name on it. Another tip:

> "As a general thing, the Japanese are prepared to treat foreigners with great courtesy and often with genuine warmth – provided that they are only visitors or, if resident in Japan, content to remain essentially foreign in their attitudes and lifestyles. But if a *gaijin* shows signs of successfully mastering the nuances of Japanese culture and social behaviour, the instinctive Japanese response is to grow uneasy and to seek to freeze him out by somehow reminding him of his ineradicable foreignness."

—Robert C. Christopher
The Japanese Mind, 1984, Pan Books.

NON-VERBAL MESSAGES

When you communicate with someone from a different culture you not only have to speak a different language, you also have to understand the different body language and gestures. The Japanese pay far more attention to non-verbal communication than westerners do, so it is important that you learn to read these messages. Make sure that you do not send out the wrong signals.

The Japanese rely heavily on non-verbal communication because they believe that such messages – tone of voice, facial expression and posture – reveal the internal state more accurately than words, which can be easily manipulated. Through the centuries of living so closely together in a small island country, with their strict codes of behaviour, the Japanese have developed many common emotional and cultural bases with each other, and the need to use words to express themselves is less important to them. One could liken this to how a husband and wife, who having been together for years, can send messages with a nod, a droop of the shoulders or the tongue moving in a half-opened mouth.

This Japanese preference for communication without words is reflected in expressions like *ishin-denshin*, heart to heart communicating or tacit understanding. And *haragei*, which means the art of reading gut feelings. To the Japanese, a person who relies too much on words and logic is verbose, argumentative, simplistic and sometimes slow.

Japanese are brought up to avoid eye contact, or to make the very minimum eye contact.

Non-verbal communication occurs in all other cultures, but in Japan it is done on a much more subtle level that foreigners often fail to observe. They assume that the Japanese are self-effacing and vague, and unaware of the constant string of messages they are transmitting. For example, when you hear a Japanese say 'yes' with a tone of hesitation, you may not interpret it as a polite way of saying no.

And, as much as they send out non-verbal messages, they receive them all the time as well. You may not realise that if you frown during a conversation with a Japanese, he or she will not read it as an indication of your difficulty in understanding or your confusion, but as a sign of your disapproval or dislike, or even hatred for the speaker.

Non-verbal communication is thus very important in Japan. You should learn the more important signals.

Smile, Laugh, Giggle

Why do the Japanese always smile instead of saying yes or no? Why do they laugh when it is not funny? These questions are often asked by foreigners puzzled by the perennial enigmatic Japanese smile and the unexpected laugh. An English teacher asks a student to give her the answer to a question. The student smiles and looks at his fellow student sitting next to him. Then they start giggling. You stop someone on the street and ask her the way to Shibuya station. She laughs, shaking her head.

The Japanese laugh for many reasons, not only when they are happy or amused at something funny. They laugh when they are embarrassed, just as westerners may utter a small nervous laugh. The woman who responded to the request for directions to Shibuya station laughed because she didn't understand what was being said to her or she may have laughed to cover her ignorance and embarrassment. She laughed at herself before anyone else laughed at her. This is quite a common reaction when you speak to a Japanese in English and he does not understand what you have said, or if you are trying out your Japanese on him. He is not laughing at you, but at the awkward situation he is in. You should not get put off or angry, but should repeat what you have said slowly. Or write it down.

A common reason for the Japanese smile, which you will frequently encounter in business meetings, is a reluctance to say no. They smile because they are concerned about hurting your feelings and making you lose face if they say no. It is avoiding the unpleasant, in a way. They also smile when they are uncomfortable or upset about something. It is a kind of grin-and-bear-it reaction. Smiling is a most important part of the system for living with each other in harmonious relationships.

Covering the Mouth when Laughing

Japanese women cover their mouths with their hands when they laugh. You will notice it especially among teenage girls chatting together. They are not embarrassed about their bad teeth when they do this, as some foreigners have suggested. Japanese women are taught from their earliest age that laughing out loud with their mouths wide open is unbecoming and vulgar – *hashitanai*. They also put a hand over their mouth when they are trying to suppress laughter at something funny but naughty to laugh at.

Avoidance of Eye Contact

Westerners are often suspicious of the person they are talking to when they notice the infrequency and the briefness of duration of eye contact. The Japanese try to avoid eye contact and do not maintain eye contact for as long as westerners do. Eye contact does not mean honesty or openness or confidence to them. On the contrary, it is a sign of a challenge or a menacing attitude. It is considered to be very impolite to maintain direct eye contact with someone whose status is higher than yours.

A child being scolded will never look his parent or teacher in the eye because it will be a show of defiance, but will look down to show humility. Japanese salesmen are taught to look at the necktie of a customer when making a sales pitch. (Perhaps that's why they always seem to notice your tie?) Don't misjudge a Japanese who avoids eye contact with you. He may be doing it out of respect for you.

The Blank Face

This is particularly annoying to foreigners. "I never know what those Japanese are thinking," says a frustrated expat. If you ask the Japanese a question and if they show a blank face, it usually means they either did not understand your question or do not know how to answer it. The Japanese rarely frown in these situations for fear of displaying annoyance to the questioner. The blank face in fact does send out a message.

Sleeping in Front of You

You will be surprised to see some of the Japanese at a business meeting with their arms folded and their eyes shut as though they are sleeping while you are talking to them. They are not doing this to insult you. The common explanation is that they find it easier to understand someone speaking in English if they close their eyes, because they can cut out the visual distractions and concentrate only on the sounds. It is of course true that closing their eyes prevents them from reading your western body-language incorrectly. If the man who is apparently sleeping is of a higher status to the others at the meeting, he may be showing his subordinates that he has confidence in them and is leaving them to handle the

matter without imposing his authority on them. The Japanese generally shut their eyes when there is a need to think deeply, as some westerners shut their eyes in prayer or meditation.

But without a doubt many an executive who has been up late the night before, entertaining a customer, drops off to sleep in the midst of his deep thinking! The Japanese seem to be capable of sleeping almost everywhere. Women have a strong sense of modesty in their sleeping position. Girls must curl their bodies into the modest dignified character *kinjo*, which means spirit of control.

Inhaling through Clenched Teeth

You will come across it sooner or later. The clenched teeth with a hissing, inhaling sound. They do this when they think something is difficult or they are not sure. For example, if you ask an innkeeper how much it would cost to go to some place to see the sights by taxi, she will make the hissing sound if she doesn't know. It is not unlike the western 'humming and hawing'.

Tilting the Head

Tilting the head often accompanies the clenched-teeth hissing inhalation. It means one is reluctant to answer, disagrees or is just thinking. It can be seen quite frequently during business meetings. Your response should be to wait and not press for an answer. It is a non-verbal expression of 'Let me see ...'

Scratching the Back of the Head

This indicates embarrassment. Only men do it. If you tell your friend who is getting married soon that you have heard his bride-to-be is very beautiful, he will not reply, but will just scratch the back of his head.

Waving a Hand in Front of the Body

This means *no*, *no thank you*, or to foreigners, *I don't speak English*. It could also be used as a response to the question, 'Do you have any children?' At a party you may ask a Japanese woman if she would like another drink and get this gesture for a reply. Don't take it as a 'buzz-off' sign. The 'no' hand movement seen when asking for directions in the street means, 'No, I don't speak English.'

The Hand Wave

You could really get confused with this Japanese version of a gesture you are familiar with. The hand moving quickly sideways beside one's face; the goodbye sign to the American. In Japan, it means *come here!*

Pointing to One's Nose

This is the Japanese equivalent to pointing to one's breast in the western gesture meaning, 'Who? Me?' The Japanese do not point to their heart. They point to their nose. It is a gesture that you will find takes a long time to get used to.

Counting with the Fingers

The Japanese count with their fingers in the exact opposite way to westerners. They start with the open hand and fold the fingers in one by one, starting with the thumb. After five, they continue by opening out the fingers, starting with the little finger. If one has to indicate, say, *seven*, the Japanese will not do this by holding up two hands to show seven digits sticking out. The right hand will be open with five digits stretched out and against the palm of this hand he will place two fingers of his left hand. Remember this when you are shopping.

The peace sign is two fingers in a 'V', as it is all over the world, and so is the thumbs-up or thumbs-down sign.

Straight-backed Posture

The Japanese may appear to be a nervous lot from the way they are always sitting upright or standing straight-backed. To them the upright posture signifies seriousness and good upbringing, especially in business situations. Remember that they will judge you by this measure, too. The line of the back is an indication of character to the Japanese, to a greater degree than it is in the western world.

Interpersonal Distance

The Japanese need more space about them to feel comfortable and at ease than the westerner. One would expect them to be prepared to stand and sit closer, with their smaller rooms, but the attitude of not projecting oneself into another's personal space is perhaps the root reason for this. If you get physically close to a Japanese he will feel intimidated and restless. At cocktail parties, with the noise level rising, you tend to forget this until you see your Japanese friend inching back till he hits the wall.

This is important. As much as you can be embarrassed by the hugging and cheek-kissing between men in parts of Europe, you can unsettle a Japanese by standing or sitting too close to him or her.

Silence

Western businessmen sometimes find it frustrating dealing with the Japanese because they are silent in many situations. A western teacher, after explaining something, may feel it necessary to ask her class, "Do you understand?" There will be no response. The class will be silent. At a business meeting, you introduce new prices for your improved products and wait for feedback from the Japanese. They sit in silence for an excruciatingly long time. At a social gathering you may be used to the quick repartee and anecdotes coming in rapidly from the crowd around you. You look around and see a ring of silent Japanese. You could end up talking all night.

Although silence may seem to be a void, a blank space of time to westerners, the Japanese consider it an important part of the communication process. In fact they communicate many things by remaining silent. One cannot really set out the reasons why they remain silent. It is complex. They may be signalling something about the relationships between the speaker and the listeners. But it is important for the expatriate to understand that the Japanese tolerate longer periods of silence than westerners do, and they have different interpretations of silence. Some of the meanings of silence are given below.

'Yes', 'No' or 'I don't know'

This is the reason behind the students' silence in the above example of the teacher's question. When you ask a group of Japanese a question, they feel that whoever answers speaks for the group, so everyone hesitates to make that commitment, being unsure of and having a respect for the opinions of the others. The teacher should be able to pick up the individual student's reactions by facial expressions or nodding of the head. If students look hesitant to reply and look at each other it usually indicates that something is unclear to them.

They are thinking or mentally translating

This is another type of silence you will commonly encounter when you are with the Japanese. In general, they do not give a verbal signal when they think, such as 'Let's see ...', or 'Let me think ...' You should also remember that their English is usually poor, and that they need time to translate you fully.

Resistance, disapproval or disappointment

This is most likely the meaning behind the Japanese silence at a business meeting. The Japanese would be reluctant to say, "Your new prices are too high" in case you lost face. They expect you to interpret their silence in the same way another Japanese would. A *gaijin* might have reacted with an outburst like "Heck! You're crazy!" or something even stronger. Such an outburst would have been a terrible blow to the Japanese if they were presenting the new prices; it would upset the atmosphere of the meeting.

People are the same all over the world. You may have been able to read their reactions in their faces. Not in Japan. A typical Japanese reaction when they think the prices are too high is to keep a deadly serious look on their faces.

They are feeling uncomfortable

If a difficult or an unpleasant suggestion is made at a business meeting they will be silent to give them thinking time. Not only do they have to sort out their arguments, they also have to find the right words to present these gently without embarrassing the other party or putting themselves in a bad light in his eyes. They call this kind of pause *ma*, literally, a space, a gap, something in between. It is not a stone wall as a westerner may think. It is to them a space, a gap that occurs in the nature of all things. The *ma* in non-verbal communication is natural to them in business talks and social conversation.

In the cocktail party social situation mentioned above, they would not act impulsively to rush their own wisecrack or personal story after another's. The individual is not competing all the time against the group. She or he is one of the group.

The Japanese, like some westerners, clam up when they are upset or angry; only more so. They will remain silent and take a blow without feeling the need to fight back in defence. They will endure discomfort without complaining. If you have been rude or unpleasant, it would be equally rude if they spoke up to object or point out your errors.

Depending on whether the company is of the old school or not, one way to respond to a stony silence is to be yourself. Be open, in your western way, and ask if anything is wrong.

Listening

The Japanese code of politeness demands that one should listen until a person has finished talking. Westerners tend to forget how their rules of social behaviour accept interruptions today, especially when one wants a point clarified. If you interrupt a Japanese, it will be taken as impoliteness or impatience, or even as an aggressive challenge.

The Japanese have learnt not to interrupt, but to store up questions, comments and objections in their minds while the speaker continues. They do this in everyday situations, not only in formal meetings.

One reason why the Japanese listener waits for you to finish speaking is that they usually make their key point at the end of their talk, and not at the beginning as westerners usually do. It is an example of the differences in approach. The western style is to be direct. Tell them what you are going to say, is one of the accepted first rules of presentations.

The Japanese will not be so direct. They feel they have to prepare the listener for the punch line and gradually build up to it. Their language also tends to use long sentences, interspersed with qualifying or descriptive clauses, with the verb at the end. When one reads Japanese one waits for that final verb that sometimes never seems to come. You may find that you interrupt a Japanese less often than you would expect because you wait for the key message at the end.

You should learn to feel comfortable with and to tolerate long pauses between sentences when a Japanese is speaking. Interrupting when they pause upsets them. Silence between their long sentences is part of their communication system. It allows the message to sink in before the next statement begins.

If you watch a Japanese listening to another speaking, you will notice that he keeps nodding and saying *Hai!* to the speaker. This does not mean that the listener understands or agrees with the speaker. He is showing that he is listening attentively. For the Japanese, concentration on the speaker's words and a show of empathy with the speaker are more important than bursts of interactive communication.

How to Read the Japanese 'No'

One American expat who has been doing business in Japan for ten years remembers his boss telling him before his departure for Japan, "Don't take NO for an answer." He says he has yet to hear 'No' for an answer from the Japanese.

How the Japanese avoid 'No' has already been discussed, but it bears repeating. 'No' is too direct and blunt a response for them. They believe it turns a person off and creates a barrier to communication. They will indicate the negative indirectly in various ways. One Japanese student has listed 16 ways they indicate 'No'. Some of these are:

silence
hesitation
counter-questions (e.g. 'Why do you ask me that?')
changing the subject
saying, 'Yes, but ...'
saying, 'It's difficult ...'
apologising
explaining that the listener is in a delicate situation

Hear 'One', Understand 'Two'

This is a Japanese phrase that describes their communication style quite aptly. Because they place much reliance on *ishin-denshin*, tacit understanding, they are always looking for possible hidden meanings behind a person's words, and they try to derive by intuition the unspoken part of the verbal expression. For instance, if someone says, "It's a little hot in this room, isn't it?" a Japanese will get up and open the window.

This tendency to read more into speech than is literally said often makes the Japanese appear to overreact because they have over-interpreted the spoken word. An American woman once asked her Japanese office colleagues, "Do you know where I can get tickets for baseball games?" The next day she found two tickets for a baseball game for the following Sunday on her desk.

You have to be aware of this at all times. It explains how they react when you have made a statement or asked a question. If you realise after you have said something that it could be misinterpreted, ask them politely not to do what you suddenly anticipate they might do.

Apology and Appreciation

The rule of thumb in Japan is to say twice as many times your *sorry*'s and *thank you*'s as you would at home! *Sumimasen* and *arigato* are the golden key-words to smoothen personal relations with the Japanese.

You will be constantly surprised how often and unexpectedly they say 'Thank you' – for the smallest of favours and for something that happened in the past, which you have long forgotten about. Or even for anticipated tolerance. When a Japanese businessman calls on another he starts off with, "*Itsumo osewani natte orimasu*" (I will always be obliged to you).

You will see them dip their heads in a token bow to strangers in a lift with a muttered *domo*, thanking you for pressing the button for them, or holding the door open, or for some reason you can't figure out. Special favours are not only responded to with many repeated *thank you*'s but with gifts and invitations to dinner.

The Japanese also apologise profusely for the slightest inconvenience they may cause. In fact, the apologetic word *sumimasen* is often used where a westerner would use *please*. A colleague may come up to your desk in the office and say, "*Sumimasen ga*. May I borrow your English dictionary?" If he wants to ask his boss a question, he would start off by saying, "*Oisogashii tokoro sumimasen* ..." (I'm sorry to bother you when you are so busy), even if his boss is gazing idly out of the window. When a misunderstanding arises between two people, the first thing they do is apologise to each other, each assuming she or he is at fault, rather than rush into finding out who is to blame for it.

In Japanese, *I'm sorry* is not always an admission of guilt. It often means *I'm sorry for the inconvenience*, or *I'm sorry that this situation has happened between us*. It is a gesture of humility and consideration for the feelings of others.

The Japanese also continuously assume responsibility for the group they belong to, and will apologise for something a member of the group has done. It is this attitude that sometimes makes a company president resign because one of his employees has made a blunder.

One form of this general attitude may hit you one day. If you have cut across standing routines and caused an immigration official or government servant some slight ripple to the even tenor of his civil service ways, you will have to write a letter of apology. This often upsets expatriates, particularly when they believe that they have done nothing wrong. It could be a simple matter of a foreign resident failing to give notice of his office moving to another building. Accept the procedure of writing the apology letter. It will smoothen out the way for the future.

Don't forget that Martin Friedman's saying applies in Japan as it does all over the world: "Hell hath no fury like a bureaucrat scorned."

Some Don'ts

Don't ask too many 'why' questions

It will be taken as rather silly, lacking in humility and trust, arrogant, aggressive or even challenging. The Japanese have lived with many systems for hundreds of years, whether they are senseless or illogical to the westerner, and accept them without asking why. The question may be interpreted as "Why isn't this as it is in *my* country?" – triggering off a host of possible reactions, such as "This *gaijin* is so stupid, he cannot see the logic of it", or "He thinks everything not done his way is wrong", or "Do we have to explain everything to them?"

On the other hand, it may embarrass them because they do not know the real reason why, and pushing it will cause them to be horrified at your totally uncouth behaviour and insensibility to their plight. It is often wiser to sit back, and accept and enjoy Japan as it is, instead of analysing everything.

Don't ask a Japanese, when he is quiet, "Why are you so quiet?" or "What are you thinking of?"

These are most annoying questions to them. Silence is not necessarily a sign of annoyance or disapproval with the company around them.

Don't touch a Japanese as you would touch people at home
Patting a friend on the back to show your friendliness, putting your arm round someone's shoulders, and other such body contact make the Japanese uneasy. Body contact is a privilege of intimate friends. Even in private, they touch each other much less than westerners or the people of India and South America do.

Don't get too friendly and informal at your workplace
A businessman should not put his hands in his pockets or clasp them at the back of his head when talking. Neither should he tilt his chair or put his feet on the desk or a low tea table.

Slouching in your seat and crossing your legs in front of someone of higher status should also be avoided. Such body positions, although quite natural to you, are likely to be interpreted as disinterest, frivolity or sloppiness – characteristics of one who should not be taken seriously.

Don't show emotions too openly
Particularly when you are angry. An adult who loses his or her temper in public is not only regarded as undisciplined and puerile, but is most embarrassing to the Japanese. Raising your voice and shouting is the epitome of disgraceful, barbaric behaviour.

Don't assume they will enjoy your jokes
After some contact with the Japanese you may come to the conclusion that they have absolutely no sense of humour. That is not true. They enjoy the funny, the bizarre, and pranks. They toss out humorous repartee as much as people do all over the world. But their sense of humour is very different from the westerner's. Time and again you may get someone to translate a joke that has sent the company into peals of laughter and you will find it odd, perhaps childish, and will

have to force a polite laugh.

As much as you do not understand their jokes, they may not understand yours. You have to be aware of this all the time. It may cause much bewilderment and many questions if one of your jokes does not go off. But having warned you of the difference in the Japanese sense of humour, we must add that there is much common ground of situations and wisecracks which both westerners and Japanese enjoy.

Jokes about getting drunk are often not funny to them, because getting drunk is a fun-thing and not an anti-social thing to them. Subtle jokes on sex may mean nothing as sex is a natural thing. Crude sex jokes will disgust the most lecherous fellow in the office as it will disgust your vicar at home.

There is also the problem of the limited knowledge of English. Not being able to understand a pun may cause them embarrassment.

JAPANESE ENGLISH

Most Japanese who went to school after the war have studied English for at least six years, starting in middle school. Many who go to university take another four years of English courses. They can read and write but have not had enough practice in spoken English and the Japanese who teach them English often do not speak it fluently. This has given rise to a great many English conversation schools in the larger cities and many companies have in-house programmes to improve the conversational English of their employees. There are even 'English-conversation lounges', where they can chat with native speakers.

They are aware of their shortcomings in spoken English. You may be approached by someone in the street asking in a charming, open and naive way, "May I speak English with you?" We wonder how many of these brave and eager young people end up talking to a tourist with a heavy Scot or Bronx accent, or a German struggling with English.

Behind this weakness in English, and other languages, is one basic fact; they are afraid of making mistakes and embarrassing themselves. Even those who are competent in a language will apologise for being, 'not so good'.

All over the world where English is learnt and spoken as a second or third language there are variations of English which the linguists call 'varieties'. Japanese English is one of those varieties. If you are going to live in Japan you should learn some of the more common deviations of Japanese English.

Varieties of English differ from the genuine thing in pronunciation, grammar, and usage of certain words. Typical pronunciations, apart from the obvious absence of *l* and *v* in the Japanese phonetic system, are *Jarparn* (Japan) and *mar-neigh-ger* (manager). Grammar deviations need not concern you. They are technicalities that usually do not mask the real meanings.

Japanese usage of words, that is, the use of words in a manner which is different from what you are familiar with, is important. Some examples are given here, but there are many more which you will pick up if you are alive to the fact that the Japanese could be ascribing different meanings and nuances to words with which you are familiar.

'Why don't you …', as in "Why don't you quit smoking" may seem like a polite communication of an order to you, but the Japanese always use that phrase in its literal sense. It is a question to them, not an indirect, polite request.

As one would expect, the Japanese have also attributed some of the nuances of their own words to equivalent English words, and they have created new meanings for 'borrowed' English words. They have taken 'follow' and made it *foro suru* which means to follow through or to back someone up. 'Neck' has been adapted to *nekku*, a nexus, the cause of trouble, the drawback, the bottleneck. The old word for a 'standard lamp', a lamp on a vertical stand, has become *sutando*. In the pre-war days, when the new fashion word 'two-piece' hit the West, they adopted it and turned it around so that a *one-pisu* today means a dress; just one piece. Another popular example of *gaida go* (foreign words) are *arubaito*, meaning part-time job, derived from the German *arbait*.

Avoiding Pitfalls of Communication in English

These are basic points to help you cope with the fact that you will on many occasions have to communicate with someone whose English is very, very basic, and whose ear is not attuned to your accent.

SIMPLIFY YOUR ENGLISH.

It may seem too obvious to you, but we cannot stress too strongly the need to simplify the English you use when you talk to a Japanese. Don't say, "I have a suggestion concerning our ad campaign for the new software which I'm sure you have already heard of from Mr A of our Sales Department, and which, by the way, I think will be one of the most competitive products in the market." Break up your sentences. Convey the information one shot at a time.

Avoid colloquial expressions, slang, new 'in-words'

The Japanese may have learnt some slang or Americanisms, but even if they have, one is never sure if they have been taught by an Englishman or an American, so one should not use phrases like 'throw out the baby with the bathwater', 'you deserve a pat on the back for that', 'the toilet's crook', 'give him the old one-two', etc.

Slow down your talking speed

Don't forget that you are speaking to people who have had little opportunity to listen to conversational English, or that you have a regional accent. They not only have to unravel your way of saying things but also the English meanings of your words. Do not hesitate to ask if you are speaking too fast.

Write it down

If the message is important, write it down. You'll probably give the verbal message first and then ask if you can write it down, and then you'll hear the, 'Ah!' as they read what you have written and realise what those bits they could not catch were.

Confirm

As we have warned you, the Japanese *Hai* does not always mean 'yes' so it is a good idea to summarise what you have said, and ask them to confirm that they have fully understood you.

One day when you are in a transit lounge without a *Culture Shock* book to read, you may see a group of orientals come in, and decide to watch them to while away the time. You will ask yourself, are they Chinese, Thai, Japanese, Koreans or Vietnamese?

Dress will give you a clue or two.

What if they are all in the world's standard businessman's grey suit complete with standard briefcase?

Body language. That's what will tell you where they come from. Try it sometime.

— Chapter Five —

SOCIALISING WITH THE JAPANESE

The rules of social behaviour are part of a culture, and in Japan they are very complex and detailed.

When you came to Japan you brought with you your assumptions about how to behave with people, all the rules and regulations of your society. Unfortunately, many think that the rules of good behaviour between people are universal, and that if you are just your natural self, people will accept you. Or that if you have good intentions, things will work out nicely. These simple and false beliefs often lead to *faux pas* and unnecessary misunderstandings.

This chapter contains some information on Japanese etiquette, but these are only the most obvious differences between their ways and the relaxed ways of the West. A full guide to Japanese etiquette probably requires a whole set of books.

It is important to keep in mind that the Japanese place a great deal of emphasis on doing everything in the proper way. They are always conscious of propriety in social behaviour. It is these rules that make them feel a part of the various groups they belong to, and that make them truly Japanese. Familiarity with their ways will not only help you win respect from them but will also help you to be more effective in whatever you do in Japan.

BOWING AND NAME CARD EXCHANGE

The Japanese meet people formally with bowing and the exchange of name cards.

Bowing

There are two types of bowing, formal and casual.

The formal bow is used when Japanese meet for the first time. It is a deep and long bow. You stand face to face with the other person, slightly further off than you need to stand to shake hands (and with enough space to ensure that you don't bump heads when you bow!), and bend forward from your waist. A man puts his hands by his sides. A woman clasps her hands together loosely in front. You should bow to an angle of about 45° and keep your eyes on the ground. Pause at the lowest position for a second and return to the upright position slowly. You should be standing up with a straight back when you start your bow so that your back doesn't look too rounded when you are bowing. Eye contact must be avoided because it indicates a lack of humility. It is like staring too hard in the western social code.

Both parties bow simultaneously. The one who starts the self-introduction usually bows lower than the other.

Before you bow, you introduce yourself saying, "*Hajimemashite*" (literally, the first time, or the beginning), and you give your name with, "John Doe, *desu*" (literally, it is John Doe), and then you say, "*Dozo, yoroshiku*" (It is a pleasure, or I am pleased). Do not forget to pronounce the *o* of *dozo* as a long *o*, as in beau or dough. The word is written in Japanese as *do-u-zo*.

Do not add *San* (Mr, Mrs, or Miss) after your name. You may use only your surname or your full name.

Remember, the Japanese put their family name first. Today businessmen nearly always reverse the traditional order when printing their name cards in English, while Japanese who do not deal with foreigners keep to the traditional form. You can get confused sometimes as Takahashi Seicho, Mr Takahashi, may have Seicho Takahashi on his overseas card. Sooner or later you will be able to recognise a surname and distinguish it from a first name.

You do not have to bow deeply at your second meeting, unless it is a formal occasion. A 15° angle is about the minimum. You say the appropriate *ohayo gozaimasu* (good morning), *konichiwa* (good afternoon), or *konbanwa* (good evening). But do not add the name to your greeting as you would say, "Good morning, Miss Jones."

The whole business of bowing is a social art that has been grossly simplified here. It is as important and tricky as getting both the 'smart' and 'casual' right when the boss's invitation says 'smart-casual'. Or in countries where the internal revenue man comes round to discuss your income tax, getting the wine right – not too cheap to rattle him nor too fancy to arouse his suspicions.

As far as we know, no one has published the complete bowers' guide. It would be a large book listing both the proper angles and the time to stay in the bowed position for people at various social stratas. It would also have coefficients to adjust these factors to your status vis-à-vis the person you meet. You have to give the bow the full works if you meet the prime minister, but the angle and the time before straightening up again will be different if you are the foreign minister of your country or one of his lackeys.

There would also be a correction for bowing when you meet

someone on the street. One does not bow as low on the street. Just a little less deeply. And of course, one does not try to bow while still walking. You must stop and bow.

If you think this is terribly complex, be thankful that you were not living in Japan in 'the good old days'. If you had met a man senior to you while you were in a carriage, you would have had to stop, get down onto the street, remove your overcoat and scarf, then make the appropriately angled bow. If it was a woman you would most probably have ignored her with old-style male chauvinistic aplomb.

Name Cards

Having a name card is almost as important to the Japanese as having a name. A man without a card is like a boat without a sail, or a fish without a tail. He is a person without identity. If you are a businessman it is imperative that you get yourself a good stock of name cards as soon as you arrive in Japan, or preferably before you leave home. Even if you are an expatriate wife or you are not in business, a name card is strongly recommended.

It fits in with the Japanese system of strata in society and their admirable striving to get it perfect every time. You get the woman or man's name right from the start and know just where she or he stands.

After a few months in Japan you will have quite a collection of cards. The day has not yet come when name cards will have a magnetic stripe and there will be a slot in your personal computer into which you can slip them and then put them into 'save the trees' machines, which will wipe them clean of the print and reprint and programme them without going through any pulping and hurting of egos in the process.

The last detail is important. The name card to the Japanese is a thing that must be respected. Rolling someone's name card round your finger or chewing a corner while you are talking to him is ghastly behaviour. Name cards must treated with as much respect as though they were living parts of the person whose name they carry.

You should buy a name card holder to hold your own cards and to put away cards you receive, allowing the persons who gave them to you to see that they are going to a nice, decent home. For your own reputation's sake, the holder is necessary because your card should not, in the Japanese social code, be lying loose in your pocket, rubbing shoulders with keys and coins and cigarette lighters.

That is not all. The little name card holder must be placed in the proper pocket. The hip pocket is quite unacceptable. It should be in a pocket *inside* your jacket.

The Japanese usually have the English version on one side and the Japanese on the other. Sometimes the Japanese wording is set out for the longer side to be held vertical. They use standard size cards. Unlike some Europeans, the president of the company does not have a bigger card than the rest of his staff.

The name card should be presented with two hands, and with another bow. Just before you present the card introduce yourself again with, for example, "IBM *no* Ellen Lee *desu*." *No* is the possessive word: IBM's Ellen Lee. The company name must be given first, so it is best to use the Japanese form with the possessive word *no*. IBM *no* Ellen Lee means Ellen Lee of IBM. The natural English form, Ellen Lee of IBM, incorrectly puts the personal name before the company's.

Your right hand should hold the card with your left hand gently supporting your right hand. The card should be held so that the receiver can read it; upside-down to you. You bow as you present it, avoiding eye contact. And you say "*Dozo yoroshiku*" (Pleased to meet you), as you present the card.

When you receive another's card, you take it with your right hand lightly supported by your left. You bow again. You MUST look at it even if you know who he is and who he works for. (We would say who he works for and who he is, if we were Japanese.) It is a good idea to confirm the name by saying, "Nakayama-san *desu ne*?" (Mr or Mrs or Miss Nakayama, isn't it?) You'll get the pronunciation right that way, because the other will repeat her or his name if you pronounce it wrong, without saying bluntly, "You got it wrong, mate."

The giving and the receiving of a card must not be done simultaneously. You'll never be able to get all of it right if you try to. The proper etiquette is to allow the other to present his card first, then present yours. But don't be caught in an impasse if she or he is waiting for you to present your card first.

There are finer points to this card exchange ritual. The seller, for example, bows a little lower than the buyer, and presents his card first. But there's enough of the basics above for you to cope with initially.

When you receive the card you may put it on the table in front of you, arranging cards to correspond with the positions of the men sitting opposite you. But it is taboo to write on them. And the worst thing you could do is to forget to pick them up before you leave. Neither should you grab them as you grab a handful of peanuts and stuff them in your pocket like a bunch of bills.

These name card procedures may appear to be a load of nonsense to you. But they are a good example of the importance the Japanese place on standard forms of social activity and of non-verbal messages which they are constantly exchanging. Respect and humility are but two of these. The Japanese you meet will read the signs at once if you are not conforming to their patterns. If you are, it will show them your attitude to their ways and you will start off on the right foot.

BASIC CONCEPTS OF PERSONAL BEHAVIOUR

There are some basic philosophies or concepts which are major determinants of the Japanese social codes. To understand their behaviour and why some practices have developed one must examine these basic concepts.

Wa, *Harmony*

This is a cardinal value of Japanese interpersonal relationships. Harmony between people is to them essential for living together. Harmony is regarded as being a major attribute of being Japanese. The prefix *wa* is used to distinguish Japanese things from foreign things such as dress (*wafuku*, Japanese dress as opposed to western dress), paper, or food.

Throughout their early life the Japanese are trained to act harmoniously and in a cooperative manner with others in their group. The emphasis is on orientation of yourself to the others around you and not on asserting yourself. The individual must be suppressed to conform to the group.

Confrontation to them is never good. Conflicts of individual opinions must be subdued and resolved for the good of all the members of the group. While western-educated children are taught to stand on their own feet and to think independently, Japanese education stresses the interdependence of all human beings on one another. It is a concept that westerners find stifling and very difficult to appreciate.

A person who cannot sacrifice his or her interests to accommodate others is considered immature. However brilliant an individual Japanese may be, he or she knows that one cannot go far without due conformity. Wanting to have your own way, or to thrust your opinions on others, no matter how sure you are of being right, will cause too much friction and conflict to make it worthwhile. Personal success is lost if the harmony is disrupted.

This stress on harmonious relationships between people is reflected in many patterns of Japanese behaviour. They never say a blunt 'no'. They prefer to present painful facts gently and indirectly. Their frequent apologising, '*shitsurei*', keeps reminding one that not only the one apologising but everyone around must be ever-vigilant against acts which may disrupt the harmony of living and working together.

Working with Japanese, you will never get negative feedback. The only way to get reactions that the speaker believes will hurt your feelings is to show that, say, the failure of your book cover design may be something that you yourself have expected, or to frame your questions so that the answers do not bring loss of face to you. It may take ten questions compared to the simple, "What do you think of this?" that you are used to.

In committees, a proposal is never launched without a feeling out, in obtuse preliminary discussion, of how it may upset the others. Objectors will give their views with appropriate polite phrases like, "It is just possible ..." or "Looking at the very worst scenario ..." when they think that it is in fact the most probable scenario! The chairman always asks the opinion of every single member of the committee before stating the group decision. Even if a working committee of mechanical engineers includes an electrical engineer, in case some fringe electrical point may arise, the electrical engineer will have his say just before the summing up.

Working together in harmony is the key to productivity in their eyes. And drinking together after work – allowing any ill-feeling that may have occurred and remained unvoiced to be dissipated – is part of the system.

Omoiyari, *Empathy*

Feelings are more important than reason to the Japanese. In accord with their emphasis on harmony, the ability to empathise with others, to have *omoiyari*, empathy, is valued more than the ability to be rational and practical.

It is very rude to refuse a gift from a Japanese, even if you think the gift is something to soften you up and against your principles, or quite impractical. Refusal implies rejection of the kindness and consideration being offered. Similarly, refusal of food or drink when you are a guest implies a lack of appreciation of the hospitality behind the offer.

When a Japanese encounters differences of opinion between himself and another, he will first try to put himself in the shoes of the person disagreeing with him and see how the other person would feel. He will try to empathise with that person. It is through such searching for the feelings of others that the Japanese understand their differences and resolve them. Whereas the westerner will attempt to clarify his thoughts so that the other person can see the logic of them, the Japanese reaction to conflict is to seek the feelings which block concord. They believe that re-stating the argument with all the pros and cons will not get you any nearer to reaching agreement.

This compassion for others in the group comes to the forefront when a member of the group makes a mistake. The boss will not criticise him, nor tell him that he should get it right every time, although their philosophy is, almost right is wrong. The boss's first reaction will be to get tuned in to his subordinate's feeling of shame or guilt and to empathise with him or her. He will try to show how he understands the depression and distress his man feels. Criticising him and making an issue of the mistake would be the last thing to cross his mind.

If there is a need to discuss corrective action at once the mistake will be referred to as a mistake of the team, including the boss. It is this attitude of *omoiyari* that allows them to hold their teams together. There is no need to chastise the man because he in turn empathises with the group which he has inconvenienced or let down. And somewhere within him a motivation to do better next time is stirred. *Omoiyari* is a key approach for teamwork and living together almost in each other's pockets.

Japanese sympathy shows itself in contrast to western styles when a friend is depressed or saddened with death or a lover's rejection. Sympathy will be offered through silence. The grieved one will know that friends are sharing her or his feelings. Quiet support through *omoiyari* is often far more soothing to a Japanese than words of sympathy.

The frequent use of expressions like '*Otsukaresama*' (You must be tired) is another indication of *omoiyari*. The phrase contains the honorific *o* and the polite *sama*, showing respect for the fatigued one. It does not just say you are tired. It implies thanks for your hard work.

Omoiyari gets to people and gets things done.

Two Faces of the Ego

The concepts of the inner man, the ego and the outer mask, the *persona*, that Jung and others studied have been known to the Japanese for centuries and accepted by them as two parts of the whole man. They call the inner man the *honne*, the true root, and the outer mask the *tatemae*, what stands out in front.

If one always bears in mind that everyone, however open she or he appears to be, has a different inner self, it helps in understanding people, and accepting that a mask or other self will often be worn. Harmony and *omoiyari* draw the Japanese groups close together, and to counteract the differences that can never be eradicated between individuals, *tatemae* and *honne* are accepted.

Telling white lies to avoid upsetting people one has to communicate with is presenting the *tatemae*. One cannot keep expressing thoughts that will disrupt group harmony. The *tatemae* acceptance is an essential ingredient to the Japanese group systems.

Tatemae must be maintained once presented and finding solutions to personality clashes must preserve the *tatemae* while getting to the real *honne*. A sort of two-level approach.

Hierarchy

Largely due to the influence of Confucian philosophy, which puts much emphasis on social order, the Japanese are very conscious of status and age differences. The Japanese language has different words for elder brother and sister and for younger brother and sister, like many other Asian languages. One never refers to a brother or sister without being reminded that she or he is older or younger.

In school a clear line is drawn between one's seniors, *senpai*, and one's juniors, *kohai*. The *senpai* are addressed in the polite form of language by the *kohai*. And after they leave school the *senpai-kohai* gap continues. If there are people in a company who went to the same school, the *senpai* must guide their *kohai* and treat them in a paternalistic manner.

When Japanese meet each other for the first time they ask what year the other graduated in to establish who is the *senpai* vis-à-vis each other, and then they can settle down to a comfortable relationship. One would think that they would put the year of graduation on their cards.

Although Confucius preached that all men under the heavens are one family, he also made it clear that every man had his position in the social order. The *senpai-kohai* division is one of many that criss-cross Japanese society: age, parent/child, teacher/student, boss/subordinate, buyer/seller, male/female. Some of these divisions are being eroded, but in general they are still very much part of the Japanese social fabric.

These are subtle divisions that do not distance groups as the nobility of Europe or the caste system of India did in the old days. They are necessary if people are packed close together in various groupings.

Kenson, *Modesty and* Enryo, *Reserve*

In Japan it is a virtue to play down one's abilities and assets. Anyone who speaks highly of her or his own talents or skills is considered childish and terribly conceited. Modesty is an essential virtue for social contact.

When a Japanese presents you with a gift she or he will mumble that it is nothing. If you compliment a friend on his English, she or he will say, "*Oseji dake*" (It's just your flattery) and not accept the praise with a 'thank you'. Do not take such reactions as a dismissal of your praise.

You have to adjust to their ways of self-deprecation. If you want a friend's opinion on your Japanese, you have to ask for it in a devious way. You should start off by saying that your Japanese is still very bad, even when you are pretty sure it's now fairly good. Go on by saying there must be many terrible mistakes you keep on making and then ask for your friend's opinion, forestalling his objections that he is unqualified to do so, by adding that Japanese is his mother tongue. Unless you prepare your friend by putting yourself down like this, he will never speak out his *honne*, but will praise you with his *tatemae* smile, for fear of not just making you uncomfortable but also to prevent you from getting too discouraged and ruffling your friendship.

Enryo, reserve, is also important to the Japanese in social contact. Gifts should not be accepted with alacrity. The first invitation to the guest in your house to have some peanuts or crisps will be ignored. You will have to repeat the invitation several times before she will take the food. She must show *enryo*. In the same way, an offer to help someone or do the person a favour will be politely put aside until the proper *enryo* has been clearly shown.

Kashi *and* Kari, *Social Reciprocity*

The Japanese have a keen sensitivity to the give and take of social intercourse. If Akamatsu Reiko does a favour for Murakami Tokiko, Murakami Tokiko automatically assumes an obligation to repay Akamatsu Reiko in the future. Both are aware of this. Akamatsu Reiko is said to have *kashi* (literally, a loan) over Murakami Tokiko. Murakami Tokiko in turn has *kari* (literally, a debt) to Akamatsu Reiko.

This is similar to the natural concept of social debts prevalent in many societies, but in Japan it is dynamic and ingrained in them. *Kashi* and *kari* cannot just be dissolved with time or with the understanding that Akamatsu Reiko will understand if Murakami Tokiko fails to return the favour. It is a social duty as relevant to their relationship as lending and returning money.

There are several forms by which the *kari* can be repaid, as there are in western society, but some of these are very different from what you may expect. If a family goes away on vacation and asks the neighbour to receive and sign for registered letters or feed the cat while they are away, a present must be brought back for the helpful neighbour. If the family overdoes it with a very expensive present, the neighbour will feel the indebtedness of *kari*, and give them a small gift in return. One could write a delightful farce of this to-ing and fro-ing of the neighbours, with the gift getting smaller and smaller to ridiculous extremes!

Okaeshi, the return gift, arises out of the *kashi-kari* dynamics. At weddings and funerals in Japan guests bring money as a gift or a sign of condolence. The host in turn provides *okaeshi*, which is aimed at a value of half what the guest has given. Today there is another twist to *okaeshi*. On Valentine's day (the old 'Saint' prefix is also dropped in Japan as it has been dropped in so many parts of the world), only girls are supposed to give gifts to boys. This is not quite right for the Japanese so they have created a White Day, for the boys to offer their *okaeshi*, which must be something white.

Kari is a serious duty and burden to the Japanese. Many of them often refrain from asking for favours to avoid getting involved in a new cycle of *kashi-kari*.

In the business world the *kari* you incur when you are entertained must be duly returned. The *kashi-kari* relationship once established can remain alive over a long period of time. If you were given royal treatment by a businessman when you visited Japan, though obviously on his expense account, he may expect you to treat him in an equally lavish way when he goes to your country.

Japanese who do business overseas understand that *gaijin*, foreigners, do not have this sense of obligation to return a favour in the same rigid way. But they usually do not let it deter them from continuing to expatiate their *kari*. Perhaps they just cannot release themselves.

The desire to repay their *kari* is usually genuine and not treated as a dreary unavoidable routine. Some years ago a young Singapore woman was chairing an international conference at which the president of a large Japanese company delivered a speech in poor English. At the question and answer session which followed he was confronted with many difficult questions, many of them delivered in an aggressive way. The chairwoman saw at once that it was not only his poor English that upset him, but the tone of the questions and his Japanese inability and unwillingness to return the fire with equal cutting rhetoric. She asked the meeting to write out their questions, suggesting that many more questions could be dealt with that way, and hand them in. The president responded with much relief and promised that all questions would be answered that night

With the young woman helping the president understand the questions, which were framed in difficult English, and writing out the replies for him, and the president telephoning Tokyo to get the data he needed, the two of them sat up through the greater part of the night. Every questioner had the reply slipped under his hotel room door before dawn.

That was ten years ago. Today, every time a senior man from the company comes to Singapore, he calls on the chairwoman with a small gift from the president, repeating his messages of gratitude. His *kari* still lives on.

Uchi *and* Soto, *Inside and Outside*

The Japanese make a clear distinction between those who belong to the group and those who don't. They use the words *uchi*, inside and *soto*, outside, to separate those of the family, school, company, factory section, or maybe even a circle of regular drinking mates.

They behave in quite different ways to their *uchi* people and the *soto* outsiders. They are more committed, sensitive and careful to *uchi* people and often treat *soto* people at arm's length or even ignore them.

Foreigners are often surprised to find that a Japanese who has been friendly and sensitive to other people's feelings in the office and with friends suddenly becomes quite inconsiderate and aggressive when he boards a crowded train. Or that Japanese golfer who is perfectly charming and polite with his foursome becomes rude and nasty when the party playing dreadfully slowly ahead of them refuses to let them play through. These are not schizophrenic individuals. They are merely exhibiting the differentiation the Japanese make between *uchi* and *soto* people. The same man would have gladly given up a seat for a colleague he works with, or just laughed at the slow golfers if they were members of his mahjong group.

You may work in the same company as Kori-san, and one day you meet a fellow expatriate who sells raw materials to Kori-san. You start talking about him and realise that the two of you know a Dr Jekyll-Kori and a Mr Hyde-Kori. Actually it's only Kori-san the *uchi* man and Kori-san the *soto* man.

This type of behaviour is acceptable in Japan. They realise that one cannot treat the whole world as members of the same team. The nervous energy required to maintain *wa*, harmony, in the group, to exercise *omoiyari*, and keep the artificial *tatemae* and paternal *senpai* fronts, has its limits. The *soto* people need not be treated like the family and other *uchi* people. *Soto* people don't count.

This strange exclusion of outsiders is a natural result of pulling groups so close together. The many and powerful advantages of the tightly knit team incur parallel problems. *Soto* people can be treated as outsiders but sooner or later one has to deal with *soto*. Marketing men and women in Japan know that selling to another company means approaching a group who regard you as *soto*. It puts up another unnatural hurdle to inter-company dealing. Sales teams spend a lot of time studying the prospective buyers and make many courtesy calls to soften the hard front presented to the *soto* sellers.

Uchi-soto attitudes also cause the Japanese a certain amount of tension, because one does not belong to only one group. The family and the company, for example, are two important groups. This problem is defused to some extent by ranking the company above the family. But it is not always so easy to rank priorities of the different groups to which one belongs.

There are also the umbrella group effects. The sales department may be one group, and over it is the company. Above it could be Tokyo. And the big umbrella, Japan. Thus all foreigners are *soto*.

Western society has similar problems of loyalty conflicts between the family, work mates, the bowling club ... but everyone is an individual and she or he can move from group to group, remaining an individual. That is, until one group makes demands that cut across his other interests.

The Japanese do really have a solution to the in-group and out-group attitudes which the compact-team basis of their society engenders. It is important to understand this.

Kao, *Face*

The Japanese, like many other Asians, are always concerned about what others think of them. The *kao*, the face they present, or rather the face that they perceive they present, has a marked effect on their ego and sense of security. It is a basic human characteristic, but it is more important to the Japanese than to many other peoples. A Japanese will 'lose face' by being told off in front of others. The embarrassment he feels is far more acute than any anger generated by the telling off. To lose face is one of the greatest social disgraces a woman, and much more, a man can suffer.

The Japanese rarely act spontaneously for fear of losing face. Every decision involves consideration of this aspect. This is why they seldom joke about each other or draw attention to anyone in public. One must never make another lose face.

To lose face in front of a foreigner, a *soto* person, is doubly humiliating. Like the Japanese, you must learn to be ever-vigilant of the possibility of making a Japanese lose face. The damage you will cause to a personal relationship by some derisory quip that will make a friend lose face would be irreparable.

Many *gaijin* take up an attitude after the first few months that sooner or later the dirt must come out – "They'll have to learn not to be so thin-skinned about this. I can't spend the rest of my time here pussy-footing with old Yamashita-san." The fact is that they cannot change. Face is one of the fundamental factors of their social system. You must never forget this.

ETIQUETTE

Have you ever stopped to think how complicated the rules of etiquette are in your country? They probably even differ a little as you go from north to south, east to west. Weren't they far more complicated in your grandfather's time? And wasn't it far more important in those days to do things properly?

Japanese etiquette is one of the most elaborate and complex in the world. And they still believe in sticking to the rules as in their grandfather's days. They still think the social polish of perfect etiquette reflects a superior quality of the inner being, like what the old folks called good breeding.

The rules run to hundreds. Etiquette books sell well in the bookshops because the Japanese, too are still learning and have to refer to them. We will only be able to give you the most basic rules of Japanese etiquette, but enough for you to move around without being ridiculed or sneered at with murmurs of '*Gaijin da.*'

TABLE ETIQUETTE

Seating

We have dealt with the greeting, the bow. The seating, after you have bowed, is equally important. The host, who has the say, will follow the traditional rules. If you are given the place of honour, do not protest. That is not done.

The place of highest honour is linked to the location of the door. The original principle was that the most important *samurai* would be furthest away from any attackers who came in through the door, although some books today say that the honoured guest, sitting with his back to the scroll painting, will blend in with the background. Perhaps it depends on the picture.

There is also seating protocol for automobiles, trains and elevators.

Table Manners

As you walk into a Japanese restaurant you will be greeted with shouts of '*Irrasshaimase!*' (Welcome.) Not only the girl at the door but every worker in the restaurant will call out this 'welcome'. There is no standard response. A very small bow would be best. Not too deep a bow.

The first etiquette problem you will have is shoes. This is not table manners, but as you walk into a traditional Japanese restaurant, shoes will present the first problem, as you will have to take them off. You will see where others are leaving their shoes. You take them off and leave them in a position ready for you to put them on when you are leaving, that is, they should be pointing away from the room or door you are about to enter. A little touch, but they will notice it.

You should get table manners right. You are most likely to make your first *faux pas* at the dining table, especially because you will start off with *sake*, the Japanese rice wine. Although today many Japanese will drink throughout the meal, in the old days *sake* was the before-dinner drink, and unlike the French they did not drink their wine during meals. With the *sake* , hors d'oeuvres are served: the *otoshi*, two or three dishes.

If you are dining in a traditional restaurant, you will have to sit as the Japanese do. A man may cross his legs at the ankles, but a woman must sit side-saddle with her legs together like the Little Mermaid in Copenhagen. This is the killer for big-boned people. Neither men nor women must allow their knees to risé above the level of the table.

You will be given an *oshibori*, a towel. It is meant for your hands,

At the dinner table. The cloth covers a kotatsu *or leg-warmer.*

not your face and neck or other parts of your body. Your workmates coming into the restaurant from an *akachochin* (bar) may do so, but they know that they are acting like peasants.

You should not try to make conversation with the waitresses or waiters, nor ask them for their names. It is not done.

Table arrangements are shown opposite; they show you what you

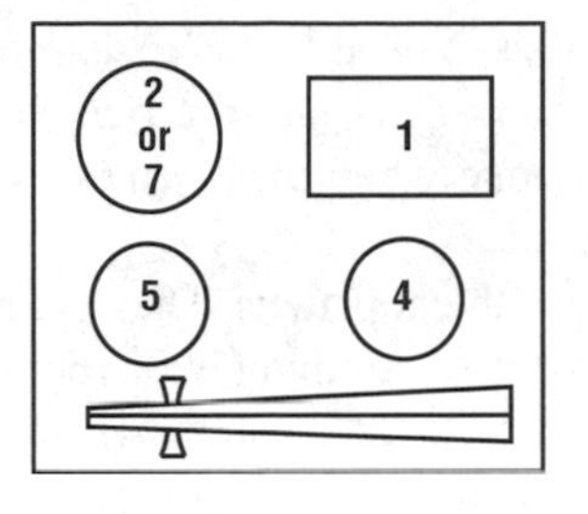

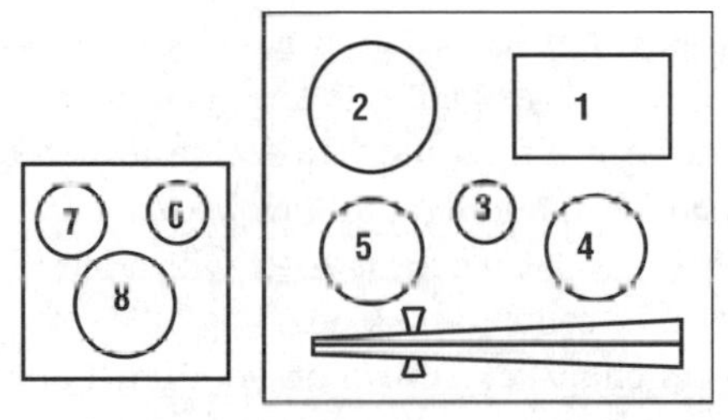

Top: A simple meal of four items.
Bottom: A more elaborate meal of eight items on two tables.
1. Sashimi, *2. Boiled food, 3. Salad, 4. Soup, 5. Rice, 6. Pickles, 7. Grilled food, 8. Steamed food.*

can expect. The diagrams also give you an idea of the different types of food served.

If you are by yourselves as *gaijin*, or if you are the host, deciding what to order, it is as usual not easy. There is an overview of Japanese food in Chapter 7. One easy way out is to order the *teishoku*, set meals, but do not try to vary them with special requests. And be prepared for the dishes ordered by different people to arrive at different times. That is normal.

The first rule of table manners concerns chopsticks. While you have all your wits fully engaged in manipulating your chopsticks, you have to remember the etiquette don'ts.

- Don't use just one chopstick or use them separately with both hands. Pretty obvious. You'll look a real *gaijin* boor.

- Don't stick your chopsticks into the rice so that they look like flagpoles. This is done when the Japanese symbolically offer a bowl of rice to the dead.
- Don't pierce food with chopsticks. They are not skewers.
- Don't point to anyone or anything with your chopsticks.
- Don't wave them in the air to illustrate what you are talking about as you would gesticulate.
- Don't use your chopsticks to draw a dish closer to you.
- Don't suck them. It's as bad as licking your plate.
- Don't touch a piece of food and then decide not to take it. You have 'contaminated' it with your chopsticks.
- Don't touch the same piece of food with your chopsticks that another person is trying to pick up.
- Don't put your chopsticks down on your bowl or anywhere else except on the chopsticks rest provided.
- Don't lay your chopsticks down crossed.

Wait until your host picks up his chopsticks before you touch yours, but do not wait until he starts. It will lead to a horrible impasse. It is the highest ranking guest who starts. The host will bow to him (even in these days it's unlikely to be his wife who does this), and the guest starts with, "*Itadakimasu*", which is equivalent to the French *bon appétit*.

However, today many Japanese appreciate that foreigners do not know the old custom of waiting for the guest to say *Itadakimasu*, and will start the eating with a bow and "*Itadakimasu*". If this happens, say your "*Itadakimasu*" and get started.

Then there are the rules about rice. Rice is the Japanese staple. In Japanese the word for rice is prefixed with the honorific *go*. It is to be treated with respect. Do not pour sauce over your rice. Rice should not be shovelled into the mouth by bringing the bowl up to the lips and bulldozing it in as the Chinese do. It should be picked up in lumps and brought to the mouth. Unlike the rice the Chinese eat, Japanese rice is sticky, and it is not difficult to pick up lumps of rice. But beware of one possible mistake. If you are eating a bowl of rice with a specially delicious sauce on it, like *unagi-don*, grilled eel on rice, do not put your chopsticks into it and stir it up to make sure there will be some of that lovely sauce when you get to the bottom of the bowl. You will break up the rice and it will not cling together in lumps. There are some dishes which allow one to bring the bowl right up against the lips. *Ochazuke*, rice with tea poured over, is one.

If you want another helping of rice, leave a few grains in your bowl. The waitress or waiter will read the signal. While your bowl is being filled, put your chopsticks down on the chopsticks rest. You must not show that you are impatient and still hungry. If you do not want too much, say, "*Okaruku negaimasu.*" When the bowl is returned to you filled with rice, put it down first, then take it up again from the table to eat. Again, you must not display hunger or greed.

The corollary of the few grains left in your bowl rule is of course that you must not leave a single grain in your bowl if you do not want any more.

There are a few rules about soya sauce. It is meant for dipping food into, not dunking, nor leaving a piece of fish to soak in. If there are chopped scallions, shredded radish or other herbs floating in the soya sauce, don't eat them. They are only there to add flavour to the sauce.

There are some patterns of behaviour at meals which you should try to understand or follow.

The Japanese do not like agitated conversations during meals. Rip-roaring jokes and loud laughter are for the bars. Even talking too much would make them uncomfortable. If there is a silence, let it be. Do not try to revive conversation by asking questions or throwing out provocative subjects. To them, mealtimes are for eating. Conversation may add to the pleasure, but it must never dominate one's attention. Some younger Japanese feel differently about this these days.

Do not be alarmed when soup is drunk or rather sucked in with loud slurping and sucking noises. They have no inhibitions about this.

Some food, like the larger *sushi* (raw fish on vinegared rice) pieces, have to be eaten with the hand.

However hungry you may be, do not ask for more of anything. And do not ask for more because you think you will be flattering your hostess if you are dining at a friend's house.

The Japanese generally do not give a second thought to smoking at the table. Picking one's teeth after the meal is also acceptable. These days many cover their mouths with their hands while they do it.

And finally, when the dinner is over, and you hear the subdued voice of your host saying to the waitress, "*Okanjo onegaishimasu*" (the check please), do not under any circumstances suggest that you split the bill. That will be terribly coarse. You incur a social debt when you accept a dinner invitation. You cannot cancel it on the spot, by bringing a bottle or offering to divvy up the check. You have to return the compliment in the way it was given.

If you are out with other *gaijin* and a decision that everyone pays for himself or herself is made, say to the waitress, "*Betsu-betsu ni onegaishimasu*." They have adapted to the strange ways of *gaijin* in most good restaurants.

The usual system is not to pay at the table but to pay the cashier on your way out. Don't forget you do not tip in Japan. You should thank your host as you leave with, "*Gochisosama deshita*" (That certainly was a feast).

Drinking Manners

If you're a businessman, sooner or later you will be invited to a bar after the day's work is done. You may be wanting to rush home or back to your hotel, but you cannot refuse too often. Even people who work with you in the same team and have got to know you well will feel slighted if you continue to refuse after two or three invitations.

There are many different types of bars. There are the posh fancy ones on the Ginza in Tokyo, where only those with big expense accounts can afford to go. Good-looking hostesses glide round you or sit at your table and talk to you with their smattering of Japlish. They ease the pain of seeing whisky at about 10,000 yen a shot on the bill.

Most Japanese go to an *akachochin*. This means red lantern – it does not have the connotations of 'red-light' – and there is always a red lantern hanging outside. *Akachochin* are clustered around train stations. They may go to the cheaper *nomiya*, literally drinking shops. These bars serve food varying from titbits to go with the drink to fairly substantial dishes. You could have enough at some places to forget about dinner.

A bar may have *karaoke*. This is a musical system which has the instrumental background without the singer. You sing to the *karaoke* music. The word comes from 'empty orchestra,' *oke* being the Japanese distortion of orchestra.

Karaoke bars can be great fun, or terribly embarrassing. The microphone is on a long lead and when it gets to your table, everyone must do his party thing. Do not try to get out of it by saying that you do not know any Japanese songs. They always have a few popular English language songs in the box to slap down this excuse. *Yesterday* and *My Way* seem to be the top of the *karaoke* western pops. Do your best. Nobody will really mind if you can't sing, provided that you don't sing for too long. You cannot refuse. In the days before the *karaoke* took over, such singing was more free and relaxed. If one couldn't sing, recitation of poetry was acceptable and often applauded with genuine appreciation.

If you are drinking beer it will be served in small glasses with bottles on the table. Everyone pours drinks for each other, so do not fill your own glass. It is a symbol of reciprocation of good feelings. I suspect the glasses are kept small to allow more pourings and more expressions of desire to exchange harmonious feelings.

Never ask anyone to fill your glass or cup of *sake* for you. It has implications of not understanding the sensitivity of the feelings

between giver and receiver.

The general rules about pouring are that the young pour for their seniors, the underlings for their bosses, sellers for buyers, and – whether you like it or not – women for men. When a glass or cup of *sake* is handed to you, receive it with both hands.

With *sake* there are some old-style manners that are still followed. The host may drink from his cup, and, after he has drained it, wipe the rim and then offer it to you. Put out both hands to receive it. It is an honour. Hold it up with both hands while he fills it. If you can, drink it all, but not in a rough seaman's gulp.

The drinking call is *kanpai*, literally, empty cup. You don't have to empty it. There will be innumerable toasts. It is imperative for you, in their eyes and contrary to western style, to join in and drink a toast that is proposed to you.

If you do not drink alcohol, you should still join in their visits to the *akachochin* or *nomiya*. You should not object to your cup of *sake* or beer glass being filled and join in the toasts by bringing the cup to your lips. The thing to say is *nomemasen*. It means *I cannot drink*. Do not say *I do not drink*, which is *nomimasen*. Note the subtle difference, not just in the sound but in the meaning. *I cannot* implies that you would very much like to but … *I do not* has the implication of not wanting to drink with the party. You should use the same *nomemasen* excuse if you have been drinking with them and have had your fill.

Accept the lack of self-discipline as the evening proceeds. The Japanese have no compunction about letting themselves go when the alcohol starts racing through their bloodstreams. That includes getting roaring drunk. The boss would not give it another thought if his man misbehaved under the influence. A rather practical approach in some ways, but surprising for a society so very disciplined.

Do not leave your glass empty, unless you want more. As soon as your glass is emptied, it will be refilled. The hard fact is that you often have to leave the bar with a full glass on the table, because it is far too tricky to gulp it down and immediately announce that you are leaving before it is refilled.

If you have been to a drunken office party, do not heave a sigh of relief on your way home and say silently to yourself, well, that's done with. They may organise the *nijikai*, the second binge, the second meeting literally. It is a fairly common follow-up. We are not sure if there are *sanjikai*; third waves.

The bar-hopping thing is also done. They call it *hashigo*, the ladder. We presume it means going down the ladder rather than up.

> St. Francis Xavier had a good impression of the Japanese. With some qualifications. He said, "I really think that among the barbarous nations there can be none that has more natural goodness than the Japanese." On their drinking habits, he commented, "They are sparing and frugal in eating, but not in drink."
>
> —from *Travellers' Tales of Old Japan*, compiled by Michael Wise, Times Books International

GIFTS

The exchanging of gifts is a big thing in Japan. Gifts are used to say thank you, congratulations, welcome, or even 'I'm sorry'. They are part of the social communication.

Apart from the occasions when you would expect gifts to be presented, such as birthdays, Christmas, visiting someone's home for the first time, or weddings, there are customs of exchanging gifts twice a year, in the summer and in the winter. These seasonal gifts are called *ochugen* (summer gifts) and *oseibo* (winter gifts). There are also funeral gifts, usually cash.

This whole business of gift-giving is fairly tricky. First there is the delicate matter of how valuable it should be, which is probably also a problem in your homeland, and there are taboos. As in many other cultures, knives, scissors and similar implements of cutting are taboo. Green tea is also not given. It is reserved as a gift for funerals and memorial services. Combs have special connotations. The word for comb is *kushi*. One meaning of *ku* is suffering and one meaning of *shi* is death. Together they deal a double blow, so combs are out.

An interesting socially prohibited gift is clothes to seniors. But it is only clothes that touch the skin. Such garments are considered too intimate to present to one's elders. It's like giving lingerie to a woman you've just met. However, socks and stockings are excluded from this rule.

The number of items you give is also significant. For auspicious occasions only odd-numbered items should be given. You have to watch this one carefully. A set of six teacups is an even-numbered gift. Two, for him and her, is even.

In line with this rule is another one. Never give four of anything. *Shi* is four and, as we pointed out above, one meaning of *shi* is death. Nine is *ku* which could mean suffering. So even if you watch the no-evens rule, you can be caught out with nine.

While you would be proud to give a pretty handmade thing in the West, the Japanese would depreciate it because handmade things are cheaper. And there is a strange measure about department store gifts. They rank above gifts bought from the local neighbourhood store at first sight. To buy a gift from a *depato* means that you have undergone all the hassles of going downtown. It has been an effort to get the gift. That is appreciated. The receiver would know at once if it is a *depato* gift from the wrapping.

With regard to the value, for house visits flowers, fruit, cookies and sweets are always welcomed. But do not overdo it with a huge bunch of imported orchids. You will embarrass your host and he will be thrown into the *kari* (social debt) fix. There is such a fine balance between over-giving and under-giving that it is best to seek the advice of a Japanese friend.

The use of gifts to say thank you is something you should always bear in mind. Remember that in Japan thank-you gifts are more common than at home.

The people close to you would expect a gift if you go away, whether it is for a vacation back home or anywhere else. Even a brief trip to Hokkaido or somewhere in Japan creates expectations of something from the area. It could be food, fruit, sweets or local delicacies. They call such gifts *omiage*. The people you work closely with at the office or factory would expect small token *omiage*. A box of sweets is the best thing for the men at work because one big box covers the lot.

The Japanese contribute to a shared gift at times, but rarely. The boss may get a Christmas present from his men who have all chipped in. It is an exception to the rule. The gift is generally regarded as a person-to-person thing.

The Japanese also have the sympathy or cheer-up gift for the sick. They have a name for it – *omimai*. Flowers and fruit are in order, not potted plants, which signify taking root in the illness. Things that are transient are ideal: consumables, things that do not last.

Gaijin who have just arrived merit gifts in the Japanese scale of things. This is exceptional: you are not expected to give anything in return. For the moment, that is. You should just chalk it up as a *kari* in your mind or in your diary. There is a debt, but it should be delayed. It would be coarse to expatiate your indebtedness immediately.

The *ochugen* and the *oseibo* will be new to you. These summer and winter gift exchanges are practised both by individuals and by companies. In business it would take some value-for-gift thinking which should be guided by fairly long-term considerations. They give you a real opportunity to say many things, so use them to advantage. Remember that once you start the seasonal gift to an individual or a company it will have to continue with far more implications of stopping than Christmas cards.

The *ochugen* and *oseibo* are usually consumer goods, such as cooking oil, coffee, tea, alcohol, soap, towels and foods-in-season like salmon or shrimp. If you're lost for ideas take a walk round the department stores. Gift vouchers of *depato* are acceptable these days. Vouchers for books or beer are safe bets.

For *ochugen* and *oseibo* there are inflexible time limits. Put these down in your diary in large letters – OCHUGEN July 1–15, OSEIBO December 1–20.

Gifts of something from your country will be especially appreciated, as you would expect, and if you are reading this before you leave home, bringing a small stock with you would be a really good investment. Include a few snazzy ones like designer scarves. Remember that the big names really thrill the Japanese. As much as they resist foreign imports, they go overboard on prestigious labels. Good whisky is one. We spell it that way, *whisky*, and not American *whiskey*, because we mean Scotch, or *sukottchi*, in Japlish. You absolutely must not forget to get your full duty-free quota when you fly in. That investment, if sent in the right directions, could do wonders. Don't try to cut corners. They know the difference between the rugged Irishes and the premium Scotches.

So much for giving. Receiving has its rules too. The cardinal rule is not to open the gift package in front of the giver. It may be directly opposed to your style, and it may need a conscious effort to remember, but it is important. When you receive a gift at home, put it away quietly and do not refer to it after you have expressed your gratitude on receiving it. Your Japanese host who receives your gift will do the same. He has not dismissed it from his mind.

The wrapping of the gift is a whole non-verbal non-body language in itself. We have mentioned the *depato* wrapping above. But there are various sets of rules for gift-wrapping that mere mortal *gaijin* will find extremely difficult to master. It is a fascinating subject and another example of how art pervades so much of their lives. Get yourself a book on this and you will have hours of entertainment, and will certainly impress your Japanese friends.

BEING A HOUSE GUEST

The Japanese rarely entertain at home. People and books say this is because of lack of space. But if you are invited to someone's house there is etiquette which visitors have to observe.

The Japanese do not think of husbands and wives as one unit as people do in the West. If your wife has made friends with someone, she may be invited to dinner, leaving you out, or vice versa.

Unless you are told that it is definitely informal, you should dress fairly formally: a suit for a man and a dress or skirt and blouse for a woman. The skirt should be suitable for sitting on a *tatami*, a floor mat, Japanese-style. If you have a friend who knows the host, ask about trousers for ladies. It is most practical. You are expected to bring a gift, such as flowers or chocolates.

In the winter you should take off your hat, overcoat, scarf and gloves before you press the doorbell. You bow when the host opens the door. Take off your shoes just after you go in.

The Japanese are very particular about shoes and slippers. When you take them off, arrange them so that they are pointing to the front door, that is, in a position that will allow you to put them on as you go out without turning around.

Interiors of Japanese homes are often cramped.

Once inside the house, you make formal bows when you meet your hostess and others. Only after this do you present your gift. If you have put it in a plastic bag, you should take it out before you present it. The wrapping must be visible. Do not say anything about it, whether it is an explanation of why you got it or how it works or whether it comes from your homeland. Your attitude should be that it is an insignificant thing not worth mentioning.

If you are offered tea or nibblers, say '*Itadakimasu*' before eating. Whatever you start eating, you must finish. It is impolite to leave half-eaten food around. Women are expected to wipe off lipstick marks they may leave on cups or glasses. Even if there is an ashtray on the table, you should ask your host's permission before you smoke. This is the old style but it is still observed by many.

Do not go into ecstasies over your host's house. The Japanese do not take their guests on a house tour. It will embarrass them. The wife's task is to serve the guests and she may not sit down with you, so do not insist that she does. Neither should you offer to help; never go into the kitchen. Do not praise ornaments or pictures you see too much. It will make your host feel obliged to offer it to you as a present, and in the strict rules of Japanese etiquette you cannot refuse a present.

Asking you to stay on for another drink is a standard politeness which is refused gently. You can stay there all night if you believe it is too polite to refuse that one more drink. You should use a variation of the *gochisosama deshita* as you leave. This is "*Kyo wa honto ni gochisosama deshita.*" It just adds, 'Today it was truly ...' to the 'it was certainly a feast' line.

As you leave, your last words should be, "*Shitsurei shimasu*", I have been rude – even if you think you have never behaved better in your whole life. It is a way of making a blanket apology for any possible indiscretion you may have unwittingly committed.

You may send a thank-you note within a week of the dinner if you want to.

ENTERTAINING AT HOME

This is hard work since there are very few catering services. The big hotels will help, at enormous cost. Some restaurants and *sushi* places make home deliveries and the pizza chains make deliveries in most of the big cities.

It is important that you realise Japanese who have not lived overseas or have never been to an expatriate party in Japan will be quite ill at ease in the easy atmosphere of informal western-style parties. And probably shocked when it really gets going, if you give that sort of party. You will have to cosset them and break them in to cope with the little culture shock you have inflicted on them in their own country. Remember, too, that houses are closely packed in Japan and keep the music volume down.

CONVERSATION TOPICS

Apart from the rules of unsavoury, embarrassing and too provocative subjects you follow at home, there are some additions to be made to the list when talking to the Japanese.

The minority groups, like the Koreans, should not be mentioned. The *Burakumin*, the outcasts of Japanese society, are absolute taboo. The Japanese are not comfortable discussing religion either. Do not try to be the prophet telling the locals what is to come after even ten years in Japan.

During business parties, do not raise the subject of wives and families. That is another world, a lesser one. The Japanese do not enjoy debate or the quick thrust and parry of western conversation. They will go silent to make sure that no offence is given by a slip of the tongue in such exchanges. Even cold for-and-against arguments on some neutral subject will not draw a Japanese in for fear that he or his opponent will lose face.

On your part, you will have to put up with some terribly naive questions like "Can you use chopsticks?" Be tolerant.

WEDDINGS

Japanese weddings are celebrated in two functions. One is the family function, a Shinto ceremony. You will not be invited to this. The function for guests is the *hiroen*. It will be either a Shinto-style ceremony or, more probably these days, western-style. Most *hiroen* are held at hotels or wedding ceremony halls. You will have to dress formally. A woman must not be dressed in all white as this colour is reserved for the bride.

The gift must be money. The norms are 20,000 yen (US$170) if you are going alone and 30,000 yen (US$250) if you are going as a couple. It has to be put into a standard wedding gift envelope which is available at *depato*. But take great care: the same counter sells funeral gift envelopes.

When you arrive there will be a reception counter for you to check in your hat, coat, briefcase (if you have come straight from the office), etc. You say to the person at the reception desk, "*Omedeto gozaimasu*" (Congratulations). Yes, to the receptionist! You hand in the gift money to her. She will ask you to sign the guest book. You check your seating place at the reception desk and go into the hall.

At the door you will be greeted by the bride and bridegroom, their parents and *baishakunin*, an elderly couple, one of whom acts as master of ceremonies. You bow, saying, "*Omedeto gozaimasu*," and go to your seat.

You can now relax and take in the proceedings. There will be speeches and toasts and the bride and groom will disappear twice for a change of clothes. The full procedure of the wedding ceremony is:

- The *baishakunin* leads the wedding couple into the hall.
- The master of ceremonies introduces himself or herself and opens the *hiroen*.
- The male *baishakunin* introduces the couple to the guests, giving the backgrounds of the man and the woman.
- Congratulatory messages are delivered by the main guests.
- A toast is drunk to the couple.
- The newly-weds cut the wedding cake.
- The dinner starts. The bride retires to change her clothes, and she returns.
- More congratulatory speeches.
- Congratulatory telegrams, messages from those not present are read.
- The bride and groom retire to change their clothes.
- More congratulatory speeches are made on the return of the couple to the hall.
- The couple retires again to change costumes.
- The couple returns and lights the candles at each table.
- The bride and groom present flowers to each other's parents.
- A thank-you speech is made by one of the parents to the guests.
- The new couple makes a thank-you speech to the guests.

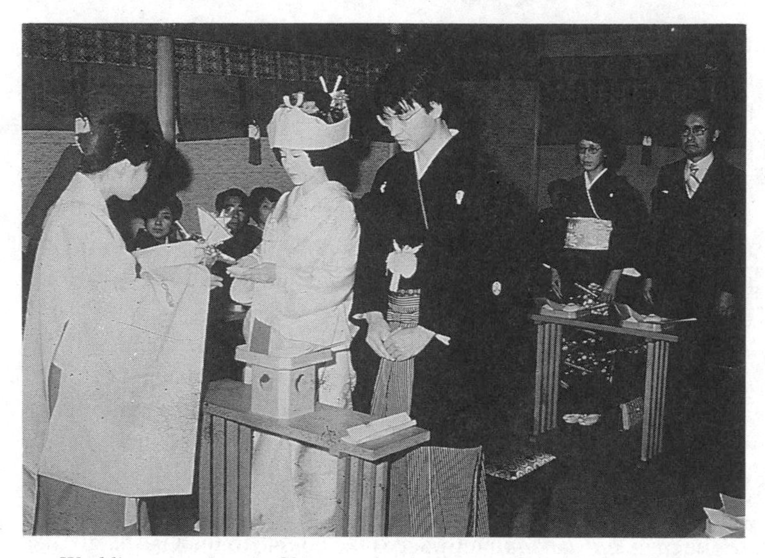

Wedding ceremony in Shinto style, the most popular form in Japan.

- The master of ceremonies closes the *hiroen*.

Be aware of a return gift being placed either in front of you or behind your seat by a waiter sometime during the ceremony. You must take it with you as you leave. Under no circumstances should you feel it, shake it or open it. As with all gifts, you ignore it. But do not forget it; leaving it behind would be an insult.

One does not get unduly excited and jolly at Japanese weddings. Take the cue from those around you if you feel like a cigarette. The old rules did not allow smoking, but many things are changing these days. As you leave, the same reception group with bride and bride-groom will be there to say goodbye. You bow and say "*Omedeto gozaimasu*" again. You also thank them for the return gift. But never, never say *Sayonara*. It has overtones of separation.

If you are the groom's boss or have a special connection with the father of the bride or groom, you may be asked to give a speech. Do not attempt to do it in your newly-learnt Japanese. Deliver it in English. It is imperative that you get a Japanese to check it because there are a million rules about not using words which might suggest separation or repetition, etc. This is most important. Jokes are taboo. Three minutes is about the maximum.

FUNERALS

The funeral may be Shinto, Buddhist or Christian. Buddhist funerals are the most common. Mandatory dress is black ties and a full suit with only black, and no flashy accessories for women. Wear something that allows you to sit on a *tatami* decently.

A money gift, a *koden*, is expected, presented in the proper envelope which is available at *depato*. It should be 5,000–10,000 yen (US$42–85) per person attending. Be very careful when you buy the envelope as there are different envelopes for Shinto, Buddhist or Christian funerals. You hand in the envelope at the reception desk with both hands at the temple or house of the deceased and say, "*Kono tabi wa domo*," I'm sorry for this misfortune.

The Japanese generally expect silence at funerals. There is no need to make sympathetic conversation. You should not try to console the family.

The procedure for a funeral is:

- Family and guests are seated. Note that the family is seated closer to the coffin than the guests as in the western style.
- Guests are greeted and the ceremony commences.
- A monk chants *sutra* for about thirty minutes.
- Condolence telegrams are read.
- *Sutra* are chanted while the family and guests go up to the altar, burn incense and pray for the deceased.
- The priest or monk leaves the room.
- A family member thanks the guests for attending.

The ceremony will take at least an hour. You will have to remain seated on the *tatami*. You will have to go to the altar and make a

Flowers, joss sticks and ancestral strips with the names of ancestors mark an annual remembrance ceremony during the Spring Equinox.

prayer. Bow to the family. Pray in your own way at the altar. Pick up some incense powder with your thumb, the pointer finger and the middle finger, bring it close to your face up to your eye level. Then go up to the incense burner and sprinkle it on the burner. Repeat this twice. You have to do the praying and incense burning procedure three times in all.

There is another common variation of the prayers. When it is your turn, go up to the altar and sit kneeling on the cushion in front of it. Bow to the family and to the Buddhist priest officiating. Join your hands together in prayer for a few seconds. Then reach out and take a joss stick from the altar with your right hand and light it using the candle at the altar.

When the joss stick is alight, extinguish the flame by waving your left hand over it. Never, ever blow out a flame on a joss stick. Push your joss stick into the sand in the pot, a little away from the others already placed there. Join your hands together and pray silently for a few seconds. Get up from the cushion and bow to the family and the Buddhist priest and walk away slowly.

Watch how others do it, refreshing your memory of the procedure described above. After the ceremony, the family and close friends of the deceased get into their cars and drive to the crematorium. You will be ushered into a room to wait in silence with others.

The urn of ashes is brought back to the deceased's house and you should go there. The tension relaxes a bit. Fond memories of the deceased are exchanged. A dinner is served.

You will receive a return gift as you leave. Return gifts are usually green tea with a bit of salt. Salt is believed to have a purifying power. The Japanese sprinkle salt on their family after they have attended a funeral before they enter the house.

Writing a thank-you note for the return gift is absolutely taboo. It indicates that you welcome the misfortune.

RANDOM RULES

There are a million things to tell you about socialising with the Japanese comfortably. There is space only to end this chapter with a miscellany of little points. They are tips which will help you get along in Japan, but behind these points are little lessons, some with wider implications.

Maps

A little point to start with. You would have realised by now the language problem that will haunt you throughout your stay. Asking directions is going to be a big hassle. You should get a map of the city you are living in. You could point to the street or the district, or even the building you have fixed as your landmark. You must get a map with Japanese written on it.

When you present it to the unfortunate victim of your enquiry, make sure it's orientated correctly so that she or he gets the hang of the map quickly.

We'll digress with an anecdote. I know Melbourne very well, but on one trip I was looking for a small street. I stopped at a traffic junction on Collims Street and pulled a map out of my pocket. Before I could really look at it, a roughly dressed middle-aged man was behind me. "Say, mate, can you tell me where Little Bourke Street is?"

Without a glance at the map, I said "Go down there. First right. Then first left." He looked at me in disgust and spat on the sidewalk, and went back to leaning against the building wall at the corner, waiting to pick a sucker-tourist. This will not happen in Japan. There is no petty crime.

Social Flattery

Put a limit on it. Kawakami-san shows an amazing knowledge of Bordeaux wines. You flatter him, but stop there. If you go too far the credits you have won will be destroyed because you will make him feel embarrassed. The Japanese are not Italians.

Forms of Address

We have told you about *san,* meaning mister or missus or miss, and the very formal *sama,* which is seldom used. Really good friends in male circles may call each other *kun*. Hanako, Otsuki's daughter, may be introduced at Hanako-chan. *Chan* is for children and women.

The words uncle, *ojisan*, and aunt, *obasan*, are used as addresses of respect, but until you learn when and to whom these words should be used, we suggest you do not use them. At least you know what *obasan* means now and you won't make the mistake one expatriate did of calling a pretty young waitress *obasan*. Remember you are a *gaijin*. You are only supposed to know the address *san*.

Seafood Varieties

Even if you just love seafood of any kind, be ever vigilant of new once-living or still-living things hauled out of the sea and presented at the table. The Japanese variety, like the Chinese variety of seafood, is wider than your taste buds have ever suspected. We advise caution, not bravado. It may be best not to announce your western Catholic tastes of seafood.

Sebiro *and All That*

We slipped in the explanation of *sebiro* above – the lounge suit. We raise it again because you will see it multiplied with the *howaito-shiyatsu*, the white shirt, over and over again *ad nauseam*.

It is a uniform. But look closely and think. Isn't it true that the Japanese are not flamboyant dressers? Doesn't this say something about them?

Nudity – and Near-nudity

Being a purist, I have added a qualification to the nudity caption because the press so often confuses the clear line between 'starkers', or what some people (expressively embracing French) call 'the nicky-nicky noo' and just bared tops.

Like the French, the Japanese feel no embarrassment about their naked bodies. But unlike the French, they do not feel the titillation of being a devil in the face of Roman Christianity.

The naked body is no big deal to them. You have heard of the bath houses where the only line between the women and the men is a rope. That's gone now. Maybe you'll find a place in the boondocks where the bath houses still have a oneness of humanity, but we are willing to bet our naked bottom dollar, that no women bathers are likely to be found there.

Seriously, they have no hang-ups about nudity. You will see the *fundoshi*, a loincloth used by men to cover the vital, but rather tightly, and it may embarrass you. It doesn't embarrass them. You'll have to get used to it.

Hyphenated Food

That is, French-Japanese, Chinese-Japanese, Malaysian-Japanese, what-have-you-Japanese foods. Look for it if you go for gastronomic experimentation. It's a brave new world of vision and taste in the big cities. The world is changing. Japan is changing. You could be there, hovering on the edge of the gastronomic state-of-the-art, or the 1990s impressionists. In one way, these hyphenated foods reveal what blends with Japanese cuisine.

Helping Yourself

You do not help yourself in Japan. You may go to the rare cocktail reception where there's a buffet, a series of stalls of *sashimi*, *sushi*, *yakitori*, mini-kebabs, and the whole works of nibblers and blotting-papers, but in a restaurant, a bar, someone's house, you *never* help yourself. You must not stretch out and fill your own cup or glass.

The host-guest code is a very rigid thing.

Eyes

The Japanese understand the full force of the eyes more than most people. It is like a knife in one's hand. One does not meet eyes in head-on conflict or understanding. The Japanese know one can, but they avoid eye contact. It is a force too dangerous to trifle with. You have to play the same game.

English Words

This is a fun one. In a previous chapter, it was mentioned that the Japanese use English words in their own way. Keep listening to these distorted sounds of English. Below are some examples without the English explanation. Try to sort these out. Remember that they sometimes add a Japanese twist to the meaning.

Remon jyusu
Mai-kah
Mai-homu
Offisu partei

Mah-neigh-jar
Rasshua Ahwar
Mochi-bei-shun (We relent on this one, motivation)
Kukki (edible)
Saa-kuru (Clue, group, geometrical shape)
Boh-na-su

What all this means is, listen. Listen to new sounds, sounds the Japanese voice-box and tongue produce. Not just listen for aural sounds. Observe and learn.

Put the radio on at home now and then and see how many words you can catch. You'll learn to listen to their sounds.

At the Elevator Door

You will notice how polite they are to each other in front of and inside elevators. There will be muttered words which obviously mean either thank you or an apology. Most of the time you will consider the thanks or apology not called for.

Just do what you think is right when you first arrive. But keep watching them and learning.

Old World Social Graces

You have many old world social graces and styles which the Japanese may not have ever seen. You don't have to make a general change, taking on their manners and throwing out your own when you live in Japan. But be always aware that you may puzzle them and may have to explain your curious bobbing up and down at the dining table when ladies come and go. Or some other acts.

You may also embarrass some women who are not used to being treated like mistresses of your heart and wielders of domestic power. If you notice that the woman is confused, or that both of you keep bowing to each other at a doorway with no one making a move for over 15 minutes, then ditch your foreign manners. Just be considerate and polite.

Spectacles and Teeth

Do more Japanese wear spectacles and have teeth patched with all sorts of metals compared to other people in the world? I don't know. Perhaps you should make a study of this while you are living in Japan. Keep looking, but don't stare, of course.

Terebi

You can watch the Japanese on TV as you sit comfortably at home, even if you don't understand what they are saying. You will find this interesting when you first arrive. In fact this is one way to see how their body language is different from that of your culture. Try it.

What the Japanese Think

What do the Japanese think of you? You American or Chinese or Iranian or whatever?

Here are some terribly subjective guesses and a challenge for you to prove them wrong by making your own observations during your stay in Japan. Here goes.

The Americans are brash and brassy. They think they own the world. Heard that before? With or without the 'ugly' adjective?

The English (Scotsmen and Welshmen will have to accept the pain that the Japanese word *Igirisu* also embraces them) are very reserved. But they have a lot of wonderful things which are so much like our Japanese ways and beliefs. The Queen is one; the blue-bloods still respected; their manners; their discipline. And don't they still sleep with open windows and thrash their public schoolboys soundly? In general, a civilised people.

The Chinese think they are the fountainhead of all our culture. In their ghastly ignorance about Japan, they think they can adapt to the ways of us Japanese better than any other people. Just because there are some *kanji* which they can read, usually not knowing that the Japanese meanings are seldom exactly the same as theirs, they tell everyone that reading Japanese is no problem to them.

Some of their food is like ours, but some of it is absolutely junk and their table manners have disappeared with their emperors.

The Koreans have not forgotten that we ruled them for over 30 years and it is a rather shameful thought for us Japanese of today that we did not succeed in civilising them. They are not to be trusted. For one thing, they do not understand the group spirit of civilisation and keep stabbing each other in the back. Let's not talk about them.

The Chinese of the Republic of China, Taiwanese or Formosans, are a better class of Chinese. Many of them appreciate our customs, having had the opportunity to learn our language and our refined ways of living while we ran their country.

The French. What artists! What poets! But what dirty people! Probably the sexiest women in the world? Though not to the taste of us older ones, their dress fashions and fabrics are held in high regard by our younger Japanese.

The Indians, Black Americans, Malays, Africans. All so badly treated because of the colour of their skins. We do not understand why. It is a stupid attitude the other people in the world developed. After all, they are just part of the inferior civilisations of the world who will never reach our level of civilised behaviour.

The Indians learn our language very quickly. The Indonesians have so many styles that resemble ours: politeness, never blurting out the uncouth 'no', respect for one's superiors, consensus to resolve conflicts, etc. The Malays are such warm people.

Israelis? Admirable people standing up to the world which cannot accept their politics because of some crazy idealism that all races are the same. Like the South Africans. Misunderstood.

Australians. Can certainly drink a lot of beer but even more brusque than the Americans. Easy to fool. Very friendly. But still quite a few war-Japanese haters alive.

Norwegians, Danish, Finnish, Swedes ... and let's throw in the Belgians and Dutch while talking about them. Good hardworking people. Not easy to understand some of their very free ways nor some of their very rigid ones. They speak a funny English. Have you ever listened to one of them asking the waiter at breakfast? It's only when you say every letter of the alphabet clearly that you can get their meaning. "F.U.N.E.X?"

Japan and the Japanese

Someone once said that they love France, and that it's only the French that they dislike. Can one say that of Japan? Think about that. You may find it is impossible to disssociate Japan from the Japanese.

The above list of 15 little new points and reminders are given to help you cope with culture shock Japan. Before you can adjust to the culture of Japan you have to know what it is. Observing them and being aware of how they behave differently from the way you behave is the first step towards bringing the culture shock fever down.

— Chapter Six —

CULTURE SHOCK

Culture shock happens to everyone who is transplanted to another country. Few are completely immune to it. It is a real malady to some and a mild feeling of indisposition to others. Part of it is subconscious. It could be masked by the physical shock of climatic change. But it is important for you to accept the fact that if any human being is transported to live in another environment, another culture, the impact of the change on the mind and the emotions causes some disruption to one's stability.

What is Culture Shock?

Culture shock is the stress and anxiety that occurs when your physical surroundings and the people around you change. You have to expend a certain amount of nervous energy to cope with change, and this causes stress.

It is similar to walking into a cocktail party that your husband has said is important to him and discovering that the room is crammed with women dressed to the nines and everyone is arguing intensely about third world countries, and the Chilean ambassador's party two days ago, and the horrible imbalance of trade between the USA and Japan, and realising that this is the diplomatic crowd that you've read about and here you are in that plain flowered thing, with those cheap earrings you picked up at Fisherman's Wharf. You feel like a fish out of water.

The difference with culture shock is that it is with you when you arrive in Japan and it could go on for months.

It's like finding yourself at a friend's dinner party where everyone is talking about some guy called 'Shoparn' whom you've never met or even heard about. You feel lost. Then you put your foot in it by asking if he's the fellow who's taken over Joe's Drugstore. You get the message when you meet his eyes across the room cringing for you But the friendly dinner party is different. The group may see at once that you don't know the man, turn to you with smiles, ask about your children, and never mention 'Shoparn' for the rest of the night. They may switch to find common ground with you. Your embarrassment fades away.

Culture shock is like this. In a strange new country, YOU have to switch and adjust to their ways. They won't. Why should they?

William James, the psychologist whose writings on psychology are said to be written in the easy style of a novel, while his brother Henry James wrote novels as though they were psychology textbooks, has a brilliant essay on habit. He pointed out the powerful force habits exert on our lives; how habits regulate and stabilise our daily life. And he pointed out how disruptive any conscious intentional attempt to break a habit can be. When you move to another country, you have to change a lot of your habits.

Culture shock will hit you at two levels. First, at the physical level. Familiar signs and familiar shapes will not be there. You may accept the change in surroundings, but your psyche has to adjust. Second, at the obvious different behaviour of the people of Japan. Both cause a certain measure of stress.

It is not just that the people around you act differently. It is also your not knowing why that creates a feeling of frustration.

Symptoms of Culture Shock

Fatigue, irritability and homesickness are some symptoms. Others may include a desire to talk to people 'who make sense', drinking heavily, suspicions that THEY are talking about you, THEY are looking at you, watching you and every move you make. Or eating at McDonald's more often than you ever did at home.

If you have children going to school they will bring their culture shock home in different ways, varying from an utter disgust at anything Japanese to a raging enthusiasm for everything Japanese. You will have to temper their swings as you have had to turn them, push them or rein them in at home.

You will have to understand culture shock to be able to help them weather it.

Who Is More Susceptible?

Teenagers, women, and those who have never left home.

The teenager struggles at home, not just with changes to her or his body but with striking new relationships with dad and mum (once daddy and mummy), and the pressure of peers at school. In a new country they have to adjust to new school systems, new faces, new 'in' things with the school group (made up perhaps of an assortment of expatriate kids), and as they take the train or bus home, or as they are driven home, they pass through new tunnels of new shapes and strange signs. They come home to a new type of house and mum may put something strange in front of them at dinner. The television's different, too.

The woman is usually harder hit than her man by culture shock. She stays at home while *he* goes off to the office or the factory. He has an objective, the same objective he has lived with in the home country. He has the expertise, the same expertise that brought him to Japan. He has the confidence of his expertise. There are problems, but he can get on with it.

She kisses him goodbye, shuts the door, and faces Japan. The small stifling apartment. The maid. Time on her hands, if she has a maid. The thought of going to the supermarket and trying to get her message across again. If she has had a job back home, the stress of the change is greater.

There are exceptions to the general rule that the wife takes the brunt of the culture shock. If *he* has to deal with the host people in his job, he has eight, nine, ten hours of it. He will come home dead beat, drained, looking for the gin or whisky or a friend or spouse to talk to. He needs her there at the door when he finally gets home.

If you have never travelled and never lived in any foreign country, you are more susceptible to culture shock. But if you have lived abroad, even in a difficult, underdeveloped country, the particular malady, culture shock Japan, could still hit you badly.

The degree of the impact of a new culture also depends on your character and personality. Two extreme types suffer very little from culture shock. Those who are alive to their surroundings and adapt quickly belong to one type. The other type includes those completely wrapped in themselves, who could be the easy-going happy-go-lucky type. The second type will not feel the impact of the foreign culture around them, but they will never be able to operate as well as those constantly aware of their surroundings. They will never learn to enjoy Japan.

There is another factor that could make you more susceptible to culture shock. If you are already under emotional stress, culture shock is more severe. You may arrive in Japan with stresses arising out of your posting there. If you hate the idea of being transferred to Japan, or are smarting under the 'why-me?' reaction to the vice-president's decision, and have not resolved it within yourself, it will still be simmering inside you. Or you may have had strong differences of opinion with your husband about the move and you have come against your own better judgement, dragging the children with you to this foreign land.

Onset and Progress of Culture Shock

Culture shock does not hit you as you walk to the immigration man in his little cubicle. Nor does it hit you when you wake up the next morning in the hotel room or even six mornings later. The crunch comes when you move into the apartment you have finally rented with all the hassle of trying to understand the interpreter's ghastly English, and everything is unpacked.

As you see new forms and symbols around you, and learn what to do and what not to do, and notice how the Japanese behave in many ways differently from how people behave back home, you will try to relate it all to the familiar reference frames of your homeland. You will see that it often can't be done. You will be confused by the culture around you which you cannot understand.

The next culture shock hits you after you have been through the highs of how wonderfully organised and efficient they are and the lows of their absolutely inane systems of house numbering, the delicious *nabe* dishes and the terrible artificiality of the bowing girls in the department stores. Maybe two weeks, a month; maybe two months later. Then you start comparing everything with home.

Culture shock may be delayed much longer if you have come to Japan ready, willing and hungry to take in all things Japanese. You weather the first storms admirably.

There is a second wave with a long time-lag behind the initial *tsunami* (tidal wave), when you think you've got it all taped, you've got the whole hang of the place, and finally you've arrived. Then an incident hits you. The Nakamuras are real people, just like the folks back home. But one day you say something and you see horror on Nakamura-san's face. You've done something wrong and you don't know what it is.

This is the second wave, and most probably the last of your culture shocks. One expert puts it at twelve months after arrival. You learn that it's not as easy as you thought it was. You finally appreciate the differences and start sorting out what you will be able to understand while you are in Japan for the next two, three years and what no American, Swedish, Canadian, Indonesian, Kenyan will appreciate without total immersion into the culture of the country.

Another little ripple may strike after you're well and truly settled in the city. You take a trip to some backwoods spot and you see another face of Japan with a whole new set of surprises.

An American expert on training US government officials and businessmen for adjustment on transfer to new countries, Robert L. Khols, graphs the progress of culture shock as a W-shaped curve. It begins with the high of the left end starting point of the W as the 'honeymoon' arrival when you are dazzled, fascinated, goggle-eyed with wonder at all things weird and wonderful about Japan.

The first trough is initial culture shock, when the crazy and ghastly details of settling into an apartment and the people at the office saying 'yes' when they mean 'no' slam into you.

Then you get the hang of it all. The middle peak of the W finds you settled, contented, now knowing how to cope with the Japanese.

The second trough of the curve is the second wave we referred to above. The realisation that you have only skimmed the surface. The terrible feeling that you will never be able to understand these crazy people (it is definitely people, rather than systems, in this trough) if you lived in Japan for a hundred years.

And, finally, the pulling out of the second dip and reaching your stable plateau.

Robert L. Khols' W-curve stretches over *fourteen months* for the average expatriate in the country with average culture shock. This may come as a bit of a shock to you.

Severe Reactions to Culture Shock

There are two extreme reactions to culture shock. One is to ignore the country and live in an artificial expatriate world of your own. The other is to go completely 'native'. Both have their obvious disadvantages.

You should appreciate the fact that people from the same country will be drawn to each other in a foreign land. It is a temptation to live a life with your countrymen, isolated from the Japanese, to bury your head ostrich-like in the sand. But it does not solve your day-to-day living stresses.

'Going native' gives you even more stress. The Japanese will be terribly embarrassed when they see you stumbling and crashing into their little private worlds.

You will meet people who have drifted to one of these extremes and see the problems they have created for themselves by not finding a golden mean which suits them. You will probably find the compromise that suits you and settle down to a new way of living.

Antidotes and Cures for Culture Shock

A million cure-alls – the antidotes, the advice, the warnings – will be thrust at you, with all the good intentions of old folks with their age-old methods of burping your firstborn. They will be offered by the old-timers who know Japan like the backs of their hands; the Company people eager to help; the Smiths whom Clara wrote to, to tell them you'll be moving to Tokyo (*A lovely couple … Jim's a software man …*).

The expatriate community in any part of the world is always willing to take you under their wing or to hit you with the mess you have got yourself into.

Listen to them. Take it all in, but with a pinch of salt. There will be gems of advice and there will be bitter hate-warped slugs or excited ravings at the wonders of Japan thrown at you.

The expatriate community will be a familiar crowd that will be comforting when you arrive in Japan. Ask them about their reactions when they first came to Japan. Sift the grain from the chaff and you will get nuggets of gold. They are people who have been down the roads you are going to walk, although most of them will tell it in the way their eyes have seen it. Listen and learn about them and with your interpretation of the way their eyes are slanted. Distil the essence of their experience; throw out the opinions and digest the facts. Discuss it with him or her when you get back home.

Watch new arrivals like yourself also. Their reactions will help you sort out yours.

The expatriates are your best first sources. They will give you what's not in the books. It's riding on the backs of people who have been through it all. But sort it out yourself.

Many writers recommend keeping a diary or a regular correspondence with friends at home as one cure. They are both very good ways to ease culture shock. A journal or diary gives you an outlet for your feelings. It also allows you to review your reactions after the passage of some time, whether it's one week or three months.

You will undoubtedly find that recording your observations and reactions will slowly sharpen your skill in observation and your ability to look into your inner self.

Writing to good friends at home also makes you recall what you have noticed, and you will start making mental notes like, "I must tell Mary how they do the eggplant." Though it will not give you a snug, secret self-analysis couch like a diary, it is better than a diary in that it will give you a certain amount of feedback to your reactions to the Japanese. David may reply with a surprise such as, "... well, the Japanese seem to be like people everywhere ..." when you thought Murakami-san's behaviour was so odd; or Mimi may admire your being able to cope with it all. Not just mental feedback, but sympathy at times.

Culture Shock Japan

Culture shock Japan is one of the worst varieties of culture shock. If you are whisked away from home and planted in some part of darkest Africa or Asia you know you will have to make many adjustments. But you will expect Japan, with all its technology, its centuries of development of the arts, its cleanliness, and its smooth organisation, to present no major problems that you cannot cope with. You've also probably read that English is taught in all their schools.

The shock is greater because you see structures and systems

parallel to what you are used to at home at first. The sober businessmen's suits. The expressways. Western restaurants with the most attentive service. And then you meet the hurdles which are so very different from those you have experienced. You hit walls that you never imagined could exist.

The Japanese have a unique culture and style of living that cannot be compared to that of any other people in the world. Many people who know the Chinese or the Koreans are tempted to think that the Japanese are basically the same kind of people, and it will come as a shock to them to realise how very wrong they were. Do not fall into such traps.

Culture shock Japan has several distinctive friction points that could wear you down.

A major difference is the Japanese use of space. On one hand, the tiny bathrooms of hotels, the small floor areas of apartments and tables packed close together in restaurants will make you feel that you have insufficient space to live in. The pressures of limited land have forced them to operate in the minimum possible space in the cities. Even in the country, their generally smaller physical build and the cold winters have made them build small and compact houses, shops and travellers' inns.

On the city streets there seem to be crowds everywhere. A businessman who works in a city will never be able to get away from the crowds at peak hours.

But on the other hand, the Japanese need more space around their bodies than westerners do. The crush in trains is an unavoidable evil to them. It goes against their grain. They do not like body contact. You may notice how uncomfortable they are when you have to sit close, almost touching, next to someone even of the same sex. You will find this strange and unnatural at first.

Noise is another thing that you will find very different. It is a common observation of new expatriate arrivals. Sales people calling out to prospective customers, waitresses in restaurants shouting out

Every year, there is a 'spring offensive', when workers campaign for higher wages and political parties grab the opportunity to protest against unpopular policies, in this case the consumption tax.

their welcomes and farewells even if they are not near the door. Loudspeakers blaring out unintelligible outpourings of Japanese during election campaigns. And the vans with their raucous loudspeakers going round even when there is no election coming up. The 'greenies', the perennial protesters and other groups.

Blank faces. The Japanese will appear to put on their blank-face masks at the slightest provocation. It does not seem to distress them as people in your country will normally be uneasy if they shut you out. A grumpy gas station attendant at home may snap rudely at your question, but he won't just stare blankly at you. He'll show emotion.

At the other extreme you will encounter young people who thrust themselves at you with, "May I speak English with you?" in horribly twisted pronunciations. Students of the English language, determined to succeed, will suppress their natural reticence when they see an opportunity, whether it is on the street, in trains, coffee shops or bars. They will most probably assume that you are from the United States.

And when they talk to you, their continually shutting you out with phrases like 'we Japanese' and 'you *gaijin*' is something that few people of other cultures can tolerate. You will also hear the phrase, *gaijin da*, all the time. 'It's a foreigner.'

The apologising, the bowing and muttering of words which even with no knowledge of Japanese you will sense are apologies, will baffle or annoy you. You just can't understand why they think they should apologise. *Shitsurei shimasu, Shitsurei shimasu, Shitsurei shimasu.* All the time!

Japlish, or Japanese-English, is a smaller irritation. Yamamoto-san speaks English, but trying to get past his Japlish to what he means could drive you up the wall. Not just pronunciation, though it could take five repetitions for you to agree to a suggestion of *remon jusu* (lemon juice), but the odd sentence constructions and vocabulary

Another shock can come when you are back in your hotel room or in your apartment, in a comforting cocoon, away from any Japanese. Earthquakes. Earth tremors. If you have never felt an earth tremor, it can be a frightening experience. If you have dined and wined rather well, you may think that the alcohol is getting to you. Or your first reaction may be that you are getting a dizzy spell. Then when you see something fall, or the pendant lamp swinging, you realise what is happening. You feel utterly helpless. You don't know whether to run out of the building or dive under the table. The very rock of your existence seems to be crumbling under you.

Culture shock can be like your first earthquake experience, if you aren't prepared for the surprise of the ground under your feet moving and changing.

— Chapter Seven —

ENJOYING JAPAN

There's gold out there.

If you have come to Japan to stay for three or four years you may have a difficult time in some respects living and coping with the perennial language barrier. It depends very much on your attitude towards the country and its people. You will help yourself to survive and enjoy your stay in Japan if you can sort out the good from the bad and if you look for the good things that have come within your reach. You will reduce the inevitable culture shock of Japan by looking for the gold. There is plenty of it.

Japan is not just one of the tourist's dreamlands, although it has a great deal to offer to the tourist. For the resident who can go beyond the time-constrained tourist limits, a whole world of exciting experiences opens up. First there is the scenic beauty of the mountains, volcanoes, forests, lakes and coastlines. And the flowers and trees. Second, the man-made gardens, temples, shrines and castles. The detailed decorations to the buildings. The beautiful old timber structures and modern architecture.

Third, the vast collection of the products of generations of craftsmen who put their whole life and soul into striving for perfection. Potters, textile dyers, forgers of swords, lacquerware painters, men who cast the temple bells and bronzes, paper-makers ... It is a long list because of the medieval devotion to narrow tasks which continued in Japan long after society in Europe had stopped breeding and nurturing its gifted craftsmen. The Japanese had and still have something closer to the wood or stone or steel they work with than the European craftsmen had. More often than not they work for the pure joy of seeing the beauty in their creations, rather than for the glory of god or some goal beyond the immediate material-rooted objective.

Fourth, the intangible arts: music, dance, the theatre and literature. Nowhere else in the world does appreciation of poetry go right down to the masses. Today Japan's ratio of novels published per capita is the highest in the world, and far, far above the second. It is a country where men and women who produce beauty in any form are appreciated and revered. Nowhere else in the world are living human beings designated National Treasures. In spite of the upheavals of the 19th and 20th centuries the past lives on in Japan as it does in Bali and other little pockets away from the mainstream. Japan *is* in the mainstream. Yet it has kept parts of its old soul intact and untainted.

If your interests are more active, there are sports, both traditional and modern, for you to enjoy as a participant or spectator: *sumo* or skiing, for example. If you are interested in searching for deeper satisfaction, living in Japan gives you an opportunity to explore Buddhism.

Finally, a new world of Japanese cuisine lies at your doorstep.

No one can honestly say after living in Japan for a year that it's like anywhere else in the world but for a few funny Japanese twists. America, Europe, China, South America and India offer new experiences, too, but there is something in the Japanese style, Japanese taste and attitudes that makes Japan truly unique.

In this chapter, you will be pointed to where rich possibilities of enjoying Japan fully lie.

SCENIC PLACES

Invest in Kodansha's *Gateway to Japan.* Get yourself a Fodor's guide. Or an Insight book. There is plenty of reading material available to research and decide what you want to see. Even the hotel chain booklets can show you the possibilities and can keep you awake with indecision and dreams of your next trip.

FOOD AND DRINK

There is a wide range of interesting new tastes in Japanese cuisine, and there are many dishes which are Japanese variations of what you are used to. There is plenty for both the adventurous and the conservative.

It has often been said that the Japanese eat with their eyes. Food is always presented in artistic compositions of shape and colour. The crockery and garnishes play an important part in food arrangement. Salt and pepper are very seldom provided at table, but soya sauce is always available, taking the place of salt.

The Japanese use sugar in almost all their dishes. You may find this strange at first, but you will soon get used to it. Their staple is rice. They eat a sticky rice that is easily picked up by chopsticks in lumps.

They eat very little protein. The bulk of their protein comes from soya beans and fish. Of the meats, pork is most common. They have a few very special dishes of beef, venison and even wild boar.

Pickles appear at every meal. The pickles with stronger tastes are eaten after the meal.

Some of the dishes you will first try will probably be what has been popular with tourists: *sukiyaki*, *tempura*, *shabu-shabu*, *yakitori*, *sushi* and *sashimi*.

Sukiyaki is cooked on a hot plate in front of you. The special ingredient is thin slices of beef which have fine layers of fat, or fat interspersed in them, salt-and-pepper as they say. The finest, and most expensive of course, is Matsuzaka beef. The cattle are massaged to break up the fat so that it migrates into the lean meat. It is delicious and there is basically nothing different in the taste from what you are used to. Even the most unadventurous will enjoy *sukiyaki*. *Sukiyaki* means spade-broiling. It must have started out in the fields, cooking a rough basic meal.

Tempura is little pieces of food deep-fried in salad oil. Prawn or shrimp *tempura* is the most common. Getting the batter right and timing the deep-frying are the two key factors of cooking *tempura*. A range of fish and vegetables is often offered with the usual prawn *tempura*. *Tempura* is dipped into a special sauce, *ten-tsuyu*. Purist connoisseurs ignore the sauce.

Tempura was brought to Japan by the Portuguese. There are various versions of the origin of the word *tempura*. One is that the Portuguese did not eat meat on Fridays, and the name comes from its description as a 'temporary' dish for the day. Another is that it comes from the Portuguese word for cooking. *Tempura* is something anyone who likes seafood will take to. But don't get too keen on it. The founder of the Tokugawa Shogunate, Tokugawa Ieyasu, is supposed to have died in 1616 from over-eating *tempura*.

Shabu-shabu is a boiling pot in front of you. You cook the beef, prawns and vegetables yourself. There is nothing that anyone could dislike in *shabu-shabu*. You mix the dipping sauce to your own taste. Sesame seeds are provided for you to grind to the degree of fineness you want, and mix with your sauce. Don't ask anyone to grind your sesame seeds for you. The Japanese have an expression, *gomasuri*, for physiognomists who grind the sesame seeds for their bosses. The word *shabu-shabu* is onomatopoeic. It is just the popping-bubbling noise of the pot.

Yakitori is grilled chicken: *yaki*, grilled, *tori*, chicken. Actually, *tori* means bird, in general. *Yakitori* could be one of the many foods cooked on a flat steel plate in front of you known by the generic term, *teppanyaki*. Watching the cook perform is part of the entertainment. It is a good meal to take your visitors from home to, as there is a variety of *teppanyaki* to allow them to choose what they want. They can see how it is cooked. Salmon cooked in foil on the plate is fantastic. The meal could end with a fried rice.

Sushi is vinegared rice pressed into what should be bite-sized cakes, and usually topped with raw fish. (It need not always be raw fish.) The range of *sushi* is incredible. *Sushi* comes in different shapes, colours, sizes, toppings, and of course, prices.

The best *sushi* are those with raw fish. *Sushi,* like sandwiches, is a meal in itself. There are *sushi* bars all over Japan, where only *sushi* is served – with liberal amounts of beer or *sake*. A *sushi* meal is a relatively simple meal. It is not the sort of meal to invite someone to in return for a dinner at a traditional restaurant. Would you return a dinner at the Ritz with an invitation to Joe's Sandwich Bar?

Sushi was thought up because the transportation of fish to the capital, Tokyo, known as Edo in the old days, was slow and the fish was not as fresh as raw fish should be. Fermented rice masked the odour and taste of such fish. Today the fermented rice is simulated with vinegar. *Sushi* bars which expect tourists have either plastic replicas of the different *sushi* or pictures from which you can make your choice. You can be cautious and order just one small plate of one kind of *sushi* and extend the order to more if you like it.

The soya sauce with some spicy ingredients in front of you is for dipping the *sushi* into. The proper thing to do is to turn your wrist, holding the *sushi* in your chopsticks, and dip the top only into the sauce. It is not always easy. Especially with big pieces.

Sashimi is for connoisseurs of fine food. It consists of raw fish and other meats. *Sashimi* is one of the wonderful taste surprises of Japan. Don't let the fact that it is raw put you off. The Japanese point out that westerners eat oysters raw. And smoked salmon.

One does not dive into *sashimi* like tackling a steak. It is eaten piece by piece, slowly, between scintillating conversation and sips of warm *sake*, *sukocchi*, or beer. The best *sashimi* deserves champagne.

Sashimi is dipped into a soya sauce in which some pungent Japanese mustard, *wasabi*, is mixed. Be careful with the *wasabi* the first time. It could burn out your tongue. If you do get the terrible burning sting from too much *wasabi*, put soya sauce on your tongue. The salt in it somehow restores your taste.

Thin-sliced ginger is often served with *sashimi*. Like bread in-between wine tasting, it cleanses the mouth of the previous taste before the next *sashimi* is eaten.

Maguro, tuna, is good and one of the cheaper *sashimi*. *Hamachi*, yellowtail, is much, much better. *Katsuo*, bonito, is rated one of the best *sashimi*. *Katsuo sashimi* has inspired paintings and poetry. It comes out in early spring.

The above are but a few of the popular dishes. We give you a beginner's list of some others below with comments here and there – facts mixed with trivia, as garnish. Do not forget, like everywhere else in the world, there are the fancy and sophisticated dishes which one eats when dining out and there are the delicious, wholesome, home-cooked dishes. There are regional foods of both categories which could make life very interesting.

Rice and Rice Gruels

There are many variations of rice. Rice served with *tempura* on top of it (*ten-don*) is one. There is rice with green tea, *chazuke*, poured over it. A red rice, *seki-han*, is eaten during the New Year celebrations. The word for the many different rice gruels or rice porridges is *kayu* but it is sometimes pronounced *gayu* in combination with other words, such as *imo-gayu*, a rice and potato gruel mixture.

Rice Cakes and Dumplings

This is a large field for exploration. Rice cakes in a soupy sea, *zoni*, is one starting point. *Kibidango*, dumplings, is another. *Mochi* is a word that, with various prefixes, covers a subset of the series.

Noodles

Most of the noodle dishes are served hot, but there are some served icy cold. This will be an interesting new taste experience. *Soba* is the word for buckwheat noodles. *Udon* is a thick noodle which will give you a fairly filling meal. If you are familiar with Chinese noodles, the thickness of the *udon* will surprise you. The Japanese versions of Chinese noodles are known as *ramen*.

Bento

Bento is a packed lunch. It is not always a basic sandwich thing. There is such a range of *bento* that one could just be a *bento* specialist and live a gastronomically opulent life. *Bento* are always prettily arranged. The colours of pickles give them a visual highlight here and there. There is rice, a meat, vegetables and *tsukemono*, pickles. And there is often a slice of fruit.

Shokado bento, named after the container, is the upmarket thing in *bento*. It will have *sashimi* for a starter. Or *ebi* (prawn) *tempura*, or *ika* (squid) *tempura*.

The *nimono*, literally boiled food, in practice boiled vegetables, would not be ordinary greens. You could get *hasu* (lotus root), *kinu-saya* (young pea pods), or *yuba* or *koyadofu* (both soya bean or soya bean cake dishes). *Sushi* is often included, delicious *agemono*, fried foods, *teriyaki* chicken or yellowtail fish fried in thick soya sauce.

A sub-variety of *bento* is *ekiben* – *bento* sold at railway stations – which varies widely from region to region. The experts will tell you that you can get (in season) *ikura bento*, salmon and salted salmon roe on soya-sauced 'brown' rice, at Iwamizawa station, on the Hakodote line, or *ika-meshi*, rice with a spicy sauce stuffed in large squid, at Mori station on the same line, or *daruma bento*, *bento* with mountain vegetables in a fancy box shaped in the form of the Daruma doll, at Takasaki station.

Go for *bento*. You can always buy your *bento* when you're out shopping during the day and take it home to microwave for dinner.

Okonomiyaki

Another series of food – the pancake series. You choose the main ingredients that go into the pancake: prawns, pork, squid, *tenkasu*, small pieces of fried *tempura* batter … the list goes on and on. If you want variations on a theme, this is it. The variations on *okonomiyaki* boggle the mind.

Nabemono

The hot pots. Stews. There is a wide range of them. This is home-cooking at its solid tasty best. Put that on your list.

WORDS FOR EATING

Here is a list of words, some with relevant comments, which will help you to shop or order meals in restaurants.

Vegetables

Vegetables cooked on the steel plate at a *teppanyaki* restaurant are very good.

- *Aspara*, asparagus. Recognise the origin?
- *Horenso*, spinach
- *Nasu*, brinjal (also called aubergines or eggplant). One dish is *yaki-nasu*, brinjals put into the fire and cooked rapidly. The burnt skin is removed by the cook in the kitchen. It is topped with bonito shavings. Unusual and good.
- *Natto*, a fermented bean dish, highly nutritious and rich in protein. It is eaten with *shoyu* and raw egg mixed together and garnished with seaweed and/or chopped spring onions.
- *Shiitake*, a mushroom
- *Tofu*, or *dofu*, soya bean cake
- *Tomorokoshi*, corn on the cob

Egg Dishes

- *Tamago*, egg, or sweet egg omelette
- *Chawan-mushi*, literally steamed in a cup. Egg, with a variety of meats and garnishings, steamed to be eaten with rice. Simple, interesting, and always a surprise.

Meats

- *Botan-nabe*, wild boar stew, not easily available
- *Reba*, liver, from the English
- *Tonkatsu*, pork cutlet. Very popular, and seen on most menus.
- *Tori*, chicken, though *tori* really means a bird.

Fish

Fish is the main meat eaten in Japan, as one might expect from a country of islands. Every Japanese knows when different fish are in season, as you know the seasons of fruits in your country.

- *Ayu*, sweetfish, a real delicacy. Dipped in a special water-pepper sauce.
- *Hamachi*, yellowtail. An excellent *sashimi*. Try it after a *maguro sashimi* and see the difference.
- *Hirame*, sole
- *Iwashi*, sardine, a spring fish. There is a nice modern cynical *haiku* which says that we in the city, isolated from nature, we only know that spring has arrived when the sardines appear on the table, having slipped in through the underground rail lines.
- *Katsuo*, bonito. Top of the *sashimi* list.
- *Kisu*, smelt
- *Maguro*, tuna. A safe regular fish for *sashimi*.
- *Nishin*, herring
- *Sake*, or *shake*. Not to be confused with the rice wine, of course. *Shake* is salmon. A favourite for cooking in foil on the *teppan*, the steel hot plate.
- *Sanma*, mackerel-pike. Highly recommended. The Japanese attribute all sorts of curative properties to it. There is an old saying: when the *sanma* are in season, the masseurs are out of business.
- *Shirano*, whitebait. Early spring.
- *Tai*, sea bream.

Shellfish and Other Seafoods

- *Awabi*, abalone
- *Akagai*, ark shell
- *Amaebi*, a sweet prawn, served raw
- *Anago*, sea eel, broiled
- *Hampen*, fluffy white fishcake. You will see fishcake in many dishes. Pink, white and grey.

- *Ika*, squid
- *Ikura*, salmon roe, from the Russian word *ikra*. On top of a *sushi*, it is not only pretty with its bright orange translucence, but delicious. Some say one can get addicted to it!
- *Kaki*, oyster. There are jokes playing on the word *kaki*, which could mean oyster or persimmon.
- *Tako*, octopus
- *Torigai*, cockle
- *Toro*, fatty part of tuna belly. A connoisseur's *sashimi*.
- *Unagi*, eel. The Japanese love broiled eels. A bowl of hot rice with pieces of eel and the oil seeping into the rice is something you have to try. The most popular form of this is known by the method of cooking, *kabayaki*. Sales skyrocket in the hottest peaks of summer. You can get *kabayaki* at the supermarket these days, but there is nothing like the real thing prepared by the specialist eel cooks.
- *Uni*, sea urchin roe

Seasonings and Garnishes

A word or two on what they use for seasoning and garnishing food will give you starting points to experiment with Japanese cooking and may help when asking a waitress or waiter how the item is cooked.

- *Batah*, butter, from the English
- *Daikon*, the Japanese radish. You'll see it everywhere, most often in finely sliced white threads. It is served sliced in that way with *sashimi*. It is also sometimes grated and mixed in *shoyu* (soya sauce) and eaten raw.
- *Karashi*, mustard
- *Kyabetsu*, cabbage, from the English
- *Negi*, leek
- *Renkon*, lotus root
- *Sato*, sugar
- *Shohga*, ginger
- *Shio*, salt. One would think that the Japanese use only soya sauce

for cooking, but they do not exclude salt. Many recipes include both salt and soya sauce.

- *Shishito*, small green pepper
- *Shiso*, beefsteak leaf, a kind of seasoning leaf
- *Shoyu*, soya sauce. To talk of soya sauce as though it was just one kind of sauce is ridiculous. It's like saying, "I'd like to buy a bottle of wine" in France and not saying anything more. If you're into Japanese cooking, this must be one of the first things you should learn about.
- *Tamanegi*, onion. Literally, a round leek.
- *Tsukemono*, pickles

Fruit

- *Ringo*, apples. Try the sweet varieties, Fuji and Mutsu.
- *Sakura*, cherries
- *Momo*, peach
- *Nashi*, pear
- *Kaki*, persimmon. Be careful about this word. *Kaki* is also oyster, written differently, but said in the same way.

Beverages

Don't fall into the trap of thinking that *sake* is simply *sake*. *Seishu* is another word for *sake*. There is a wide range of *sake*. Some are drunk chilled. There is a sweet *amazake*, and local brews known as *jizake*. *Mirin* is a sweetened *sake* but is only used for cooking.

There is a special *sake* known as *iwana-no-honezake*. The *iwana* fish, the *char*, a fish of mountain streams, is grilled, then hot *sake* is poured over it. The *sake* is drunk heavy with the flavour of the fish.

Ignore the stories they tell you that *sake* was originally made by chewing rice and spitting it out soaked in saliva to start the fermentation. That was in the very old times.

Shochu, a pungent, strong-smelling, potent distilled liquor, was originally from Kyushu. Some say the potato *shochu* is the best. A highly successful advertising campaign has brought the local Kyushu product into the all-Japan market. It cut into the whisky and gin market. If you like gin you'll like *shochu*.

Awamori is a wine originally made from millet, but now it is made from rice. It is a distilled liquor. Be warned that it is stronger than *shochu*.

Teas

Many, many books have been written on tea. If you are a tea aficionado, ask about Japanese tea, and open up a new world for yourself. You'll leave the *maccha*, the coarse green tea, far behind you after you graduate to really good teas. Don't forget that the character for tea is really just *cha*. The common word *ocha* has the honourable prefix *o* in front of it. It merits the honour.

The tea ceremony, performed to strict rituals.

Alternatives to Liquor and Tea?

The Japanese have no other drinks to shout about. Rice wines and tea have enough variations. There's always Coke, of course.

FESTIVALS

You must stir yourself and make the effort of facing the crowds to go to at least one festival. Do it early in your stay. Attending one festival may lead you to many others. There is such a variety of them. You will see many new facets of the Japanese character at these festivals.

Bon or O-Bon Festival *(13–15 July)*

This is one of the biggest festivals, and it happens all over the country. It arises out of the Buddhist belief that the eighth lunar month is when the spirits of the dead come back to earth. From a custom of going around the village houses in the 14th century to offer prayers and do ritual dances, it has become a summer festival of dancing and lanterns.

Candles and lanterns floating on rivers and lakes, with fireworks these days, light the way for the spirits to return to the paradises or hells they came from. The cynics would say that the festival is organised to send them back home, rather than welcome them.

In temples and graveyards, flickering lights bring an atmosphere of quiet eeriness and subdued festivity, but in the village squares, towers are set up for drummers and perhaps a band to pound out a rhythm all night. Everyone dances with simple hand and feet movements in concentric circles round the tower, repeating the same movements for hours on end, wrapped in a trance of the drumbeats and the summer air.

Hinamatsuri *(3 March)*

Hinamatsuri is the girls' day. Literally, it is the doll's festival. The family's treasured doll collection is brought out and displayed on tiered shelves, with the Emperor and Empress dolls on the top tier.

Hinamatsuri *collections like these are prized by the family, not just the girls.*

The display is often accompanied by exquisite miniature furniture and food replicas. The display stands for two weeks.

A sweet and mild *sake* is drunk. The girls of the family play hostess to the boys and friends who visit them on *Hinamatsuri*.

Namahage (31 December)

Namahage, celebrated at the Akagami shrine in Oga Peninsula, Akita prefecture, is a curious mixture of a harvest festival and an orgy of scaring the wits out of little children to ensure their obedience to their parents in the year ahead. After prayers in front of a bonfire, young single men – disguised as devils in straw cloaks and trousers, frightening masks and with bells around their waists – carry a wooden pail and a kitchen knife and go from house to house, knocking on doors and asking loudly, "Are there any good-for-nothing children around here?"

They are invited in and given rice cakes and *sake*. It must be tremendous fun for the young men, and a nightmare for the little ones.

These are just three of the many festivals of Japan. Get the Kodansha book on festivals and choose which ones you want to go to. There is something for everybody.

THE ARTS

Theatre and Dance

Kabuki, Noh *and* Bunraku *(puppet pheatre)*

It is impossible tell you everything about the Japanese classical theatre-dance-opera of *noh* plays and *kabuki* in this book. There is too much to tell. But you may be tempted by what Ezra Pound has said on the subject: "*Noh* is unquestionably one of the greatest arts of the world, and is quite possibly one of the most recondite [illegible] The art of allusion, or this love of allusion in art, is at the root of *noh*."

A curious quirk of history we mentioned earlier is the role a *gaijin*, Ernest Fenollosa, played in the revival of *noh*. He went to Japan as a professor of economics. He stumbled upon *noh*, which the Japanese had cast aside, and unearthed a treasure of their past. He ended his life as Imperial Commissioner of Arts in Japan. Ezra Pound describes his life as "the romance par excellence of modern scholarship."

The three characters that make up *kabuki* are song, dance and skill. Like Shakespeare and opera, or whisky, it needs study and getting over the initial natural distaste. One has to know something about the stage set-up, the elaborate props, the strange glances of the actors, and the standard audience expressions of their reactions, to savour *kabuki* fully. But like Shakespeare, opera and whisky, once you get the taste for it, it is wonderful.

Kabuki plots revolve around the elevation of a commoner to a higher status, people changing forms, women changing into men,

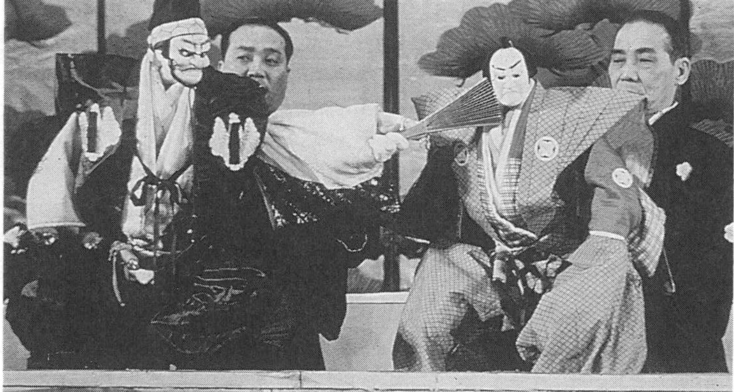

Top: Kabuki, *a traditional stage drama where all roles are played by men.*
Bottom: Bunraku, *traditional Japanese puppet theatre.*

incredible sword fights, lovers' suicide pacts and the terrible Japanese insult of hitting someone with a slipper. A point of interest is that *kabuki* actors, including those who play female roles, are male.

The amazing mechanisms of the original puppets of *bunraku* alone are interesting. The puppet theatre itself will be something new to you. It is streets ahead of the simple *Punch and Judy* shows.

Then there is *kyogen*, the comic interlude, like cartoons with punch lines on human characteristics.

Butoh

This modern dance form may interest you. It is a melding of the traditional *kabuki*, primitive dances and modern American dance. In contrast to the elaborate make-up of *kabuki*, *butoh* dancers have their bodies and faces painted white. It's not facial expressions they want to bring out, but the human body, static and in motion. They emerge from the darkness sometimes, symbolising emerging from the earth. The Sankai Juku group dances *butoh*. The man leading the group describes *butoh* as 'primitive energy'.

Japanese Painting

So very different from western brush painting, this is executed in a style that does not allow one to correct the strokes made on first impulse. The background is left blank so that all attention is focussed on the main brush lines.

Paper

The Japanese appreciation for texture, so evident in their architecture, landscaping, fabrics and ceramics, shows itself in their feel for paper as a material man can create and vary to his taste. Learn about the art of paper-making. Or learn about, and master, the finger control of paper-folding. Collect Japanese scissor-cut pictures, *kirie*.

At a more practical level, get down to the complex nuances of wrapping gifts in different papers with different styles to fit the season, the occasion, the gift, the giver and the receiver. Read about the paper masters, Furuta Kozo and Kyoko Ibe.

Fabric Dyeing and Printing

A world of its own. There is a lovely little part in a novel by one of the greatest women writers, Enchi Fumiko, where a dyer of cloth walks around the hill forests in the fall to look at the leaf colours, to find the exact hue he wants for a particular red-brown cloth. It reveals the complete devotion to the art, whether it is sword making, carp breeding, or casting of metal sculptures that the Japanese artist immerses himself or herself in.

Read about Chiba Yoshino, the Hiroshige Blue indigo dyer. Look for the beautiful intricate works of Minakawa Gekka or Moriguchi Kako.

Lacquerware

The English language adopted two words for two groups of beautiful things: *china*, for porcelain and *japanning*, for laying on lacquer, because these two countries excelled in these crafts.

You cannot live in Japan without seeing masterpieces of lacquerwork. If you start getting interested in *urushi* (lacquerwork) you could get hooked. Look for the works of Matsuda Gonroku, who has the dubious distinction of exciting Hitler with his work because Hitler saw its military applications, Furuhei Kohei, and Kokon Shoichi. You will not see the dedication of others who back up the masters: men like Kami Kimio, devoted to planting the *urushi* trees that produce the resins, and Kobayashi Yukio, the undercoater striving for perfection in his narrow craft.

Kites

Any kite enthusiast will tell you that Japanese kites are something special. If kites are your game, or if you have never ever thought about kites, look for Japanese kites.

The Suwa shrine festival in Hamamatsu, Shizuoka, includes a big kite fight at Nakatajima beach. It began in 1550 when a feudal lord announced the birth of his son with a 20th century advertiser's flair by flying a kite with his newborn son's name on it.

Today, about 60 teams attempt to cut each other's kite strings with the abrasive strings of their own kites in a tumult of shouting, leaping, jostling, laughter and a riot of colour. The occasion has all the tension of a football final and the gaiety of a Latin fiesta.

Literature

Japanese literature is as rich as the literary heritage of the English language. But the records of early literature are very limited compared to those of Latin, Greek and Chinese.

Poetry is part of their lives

In the old days gentleman lovers would be expected to send their lady a poem the next morning. The smoother ones would write an acrostic poem and the really dashing ones would sweep her off her feet with double-acrostics.

You don't know what an acrostic poem is? Well here's an example in English:

Acrostic odes like the Japanese tank**A**
Create emotions deeply eroti**C**
Racing her bloodstream with raging feve**R**
Outpourings in an endless crescend**O**
Surging with love and the music of word**S**
Touching her core with that symbol, pures**T**
Image of snow on top of Mount Fuj**I**
Climaxing with the double-acrosti**C**

Every year a poetry competition is judged on the Emperor's birthday. Thousands of poems are submitted in this national event.

The *haiku*, a 3-line, 17-syllable poem, is the most popular form of poetry. The 31-syllable poem, *tanka*, is another.

Modern writing

Modern writing is vigorous, and constantly exploring new forms. Read Murakami Hiroko, for example. Before the Pacific War the influence of Europe, particularly France, was very marked. It still influences present-day Japanese poetry. Earlier, it was pointed out that Japan has by far the highest ratio of novels published to population in the world, and from such a base the finest writers of any country would be able to surface, honed and polished by competition. Names like Kawabata and Mishima are known in the West but there are so many other brilliant writers with slants that are so very different from those of the West, including Spanish language writers.

But poetry and prose can be read and appreciated a thousand miles away. Living in Japan, your appreciation of present-day novels may be enhanced, and visits to places connected with great works and authors will add to your experience. Reading Japanese literature will help in reducing cultural shock. But altogether, sitting at home reading Japanese writing may be a waste of your time, when you can be out there in the thick of it getting the feel of Japan instead.

Modern Pottery

Ceramics is one of the areas in which Japan and the world have had a free-flowing mutual interchange of inspiration in this century. Bernard Leach is one example of a man who not only brought to England what he learnt of Japanese ceramics, but also gave new inspiration to modern Japanese potters. There are many others. The purity of Japanese painting appears in modern pottery. Simple forms, lines and colours come through with force in so much of their ceramics.

Show-Ya, a Japanese women's rock group, has had successful concerts in London, the USA and Mexico.

Music

It will take much effort to get into Japanese music, probably as much effort as for an Acid-house fan to get into Chopin. And it will need tolerance to keep an even keel when Japanese music is thrust at you. But there is beauty somewhere there, which is beauty to them and therefore not to be dismissed.

Japanese pop, on the other hand, is absolutely terrific. It has a different streak. If that's your beat, go for it. You will discover new dimensions of modern music. Japanese pop musicians have hit the top of the world on many different stages. Even if you are not a pop fan, buy a popular album and listen to new sounds. They are international – but with a Japanese touch.

Architecture

There are hundreds of temples, shrines, castles, gates, and houses of staggering beauty. And gardens: gardens laid out to induce calm on those who walk through them or who sit in silence taking it all in.

Many of the architectural masterpieces have been rebuilt, copying the originals faithfully from archive drawings and descriptions, after they were destroyed by fire or earthquakes. And many of them are steeped in history.

The Golden Pavilion, Kinkakuji, one of hundreds of examples of the beauty of Japanese architecture and landscaping. Originally the villa of a court noble, it was turned into a Buddhist temple. The gardens were laid out in 1394.

Castles

If history or architecture interests you, the many castles with a wide range of design styles should top your priority list.

Castles in Japan were not only fortresses, but became in later years symbols of power of the lord of the castle. They were thus designed with not only a functional objective but also to create strong visual impact on the people, or any rival who considered challenging the *daimyo* who held the castle. The influence of changing weapons like fire-arrows and guns, which came in from Europe in 1543, of earthquakes and the steepness of volcanic hill slopes, and superstitions that precluded towers with an even number of floors in the design of castles, is fascinating.

Some of the finest castles are:

- Himeji-jo (*jo* is castle), also known as Shirasagi-jo (White Heron Castle), built in 1609 by the son-in-law of Tokugawa Ieyasu, towering above its surroundings like a great white bird in flight.
- Osaka Castle, built by the Tokugawas on the same site as a castle built by the Toyotomi family, after it was deliberately destroyed to symbolise the end of an era steeped in history.
- Matsumoto Castle with its Tsukimi (moon viewing) tower.
- The Edo Castle ruins. Edo Castle, home of the Tokugawa *shogun*, was once the largest castle in Japan.
- Nagoya Castle, which they say is like a cat hiding its sharp claws.
- Kumamoto Castle, Wakayama Castle, Fukuyama Castle (Hiroshima prefecture), Kochi Castle (Shikoku).

Sports

Golf

If you're not the chief executive or somewhere in that lofty plane you should forget about golfing in Japan – unless you're one of those fanatics who simply cannot. Golfing is very expensive, and nearly inaccessible to mere mortals. If you live in Tokyo you will have to get up at five o'clock in the morning and drive for hours if and when some president of a large company invites you to one of the best courses outside Tokyo.

There are many driving ranges. You may have seen one or two on your way into Tokyo from Narita. Keeping your drive up to standard will not be a big problem. And there are also putting places. But muscling into a golf club requires extraordinary contacts and finances. Such excursions into the outer space of social-sporting Japan are beyond the down-to-earth scope of this book.

Sumo, *Japanese wrestling*

This is traditional Japanese wrestling. There's no way you can get into it, but it is a spectator sport that grips one as boxing, baseball or soccer does. A few years ago the entertainment world was startled to see how it shot up in television ratings as soon as it was introduced by a British television station. In Japan the English language newspapers and a radio station, Eagle 810 on AFN (Armed Forces Network) Tokyo (formerly Far East Network), will give you all the *sumo* news.

It is a national skill going back 2000 years. To get into *sumo* a boy has to join a 'stable', a *heya*, at 15 and undergo a gruelling period of discipline and training. The wrestling is done in a ring 4.55 metres in diameter. The rules are simple. The loser is the first to touch the

ground with any part of his body other than his feet, or to be thrown out of the ring. Ancient Shinto rituals and rules are interwoven into the complex protocol of *sumo*.

Sumo wrestlers are huge, obese-looking men. They wrestle almost naked but the little they wear has its standard forms. At first sight, the *sumo* wrestler is an ugly hunk of a man. But somehow westerners have taken to following *sumo* as avidly as the Japanese.

Yakyu, *baseball*

The one single western sport that the Japanese took on and made a part of their modern culture is baseball. There are still backwaters in the mountainous regions of Japan, relatively untouched by modern developments, but baseball madness has reached even there. If you're a baseball fan you will have hours and hours of pleasure watching baseball. Many American baseball players have been brought to Japan, but somehow the style of play did not bring out the best in them. You may want to investigate this statement.

Sandlot baseball: neighbourhood teams enjoy a match.

Skiing

Heavy snowfalls occur in the winter in the northern parts of Japan and the Japanese have taken to skiing like ducks to water. There are many ski slopes and organisations that will offer you a complete package of transportation, skiing equipment and accommodation. The Chubu region has the highest mountains but Hokkaido can offer you relatively uncrowded slopes with excellent powder snow. Niseko in Hokkaido has five ski slopes and 35 ski lifts. The season is late November to April. Zao in Tohoku has the finest skiing. Trees covered with ice in the winter add a different touch to the scenery. In Tohoku's Gassan ski area one can ski from April 20 to early July.

In Chubu, Hakkone and Hakuba are the popular spots. Nagano has been chosen as the site for the next winter olympics in 1998, the second to be held in Japan. The first was at Sapporo.

Tennisu, tennis

Tennis is definitely in, and will stay 'in' for a long time. You should have no difficulty finding friends to play with.

Night Life

You'll find a hundred variations on the old theme. Hotel brochures for tourists will give you the usual information. The magazine *Joyful* may have more. If you're in Tokyo and have the cash to blow, the entertainment is yours in Shinjuku and Roppongi. Don't forget that when the striptease started in the USA and the world went mad over it, after World War II it came to Tokyo and the Japanese extended it to a whole chorus line of strippers. Not just their groupy tendency, but a fresh marketing approach.

Japanese Chess – Shogi

Make yourself popular with your Japanese friends by learning *shogi*, their version of chess. It is one of the cheapest ways to get into something Japanese.

In many parts of the world there are beautiful and enchanting things: the dancers of Thailand, the traditional painters of Bali, the silversmiths of Malaysia, the poets of Bengal, the Cognac blenders of France ... but in Japan the range of arts and crafts perfected by men and women who put their whole lives and souls into their chosen field with such intense passion and concentration on detail, is extraordinary. We have touched upon some subjects which an expatriate in Japan can draw much pleasure from. There is so much more which is impossible for a tourist to appreciate and fully enjoy. You have exciting worlds at your feet.

— Chapter Eight —

DOING BUSINESS WITH THE JAPANESE

The Japanese business scene is another scene in which the surprises could cause you a great deal of stress.

Only the major surprises will be pointed out here, but they will reduce your cultural shock if you were caught up in all the rushing around of moving to Japan, and have had no time to read up on doing business there. If you're a spouse accompanying a business person to Japan, this outline of the business world will help you to understand the stresses he or she has to face.

The macro-structure of the private sector, the micro-structures within firms, and the behaviour norms and etiquette are all different from western systems. The Japanese business world, if you have not read anything about it, could be a major generator of culture shock.

The Japanese Business World

We first paint the scene in broad, generalised brush-sweeps. They give you a backdrop.

Japan is a rugged country with very little agricultural land and negligible minerals. Almost all the raw materials used by industry are imported, and this pressure has pushed Japanese industrial producers to add the maximum value possible to their finished goods. It means concentrating on productivity and technology.

The working population is limited. Human resources had to be optimised by intensive training. Immigrant labour is intolerable to them. But, in spite of controls, migrant workers have slipped in over the years, and are beginning to present the same problems as they do in Switzerland, Germany and Singapore.

The population is largely homogeneous, and crowded together. They therefore have large domestic markets that do not require long hauls for delivery. There is only one time zone in Japan. There is one language. Communication is excellent. These market factors bred mass-production units.

The stress on the group which pervades all Japanese culture dominates the business world. The firm is regarded as a family, and the same loyalty that binds families together binds the employees of companies. The firm is one unit of the umbrella group of Japan. The common goal of labour and capital has suppressed the potential conflict of labour and management in a tight labour market. Workers' loyalty to their company, and knowledge that the paternalistic firm would always look after them, prevented the merry-go-round of job-hopping from developing, in spite of labour demand exceeding supply. In the year ending 31 March 1989, only 4.2% of Japan's 59 million workers changed jobs.

Loyalty to one firm, like loyalty to one football team, engendered fierce competition towards other firms. It sharpened both their production and marketing cutting edges. Yet the group spirit brings them together when they face competition from those outside their system: the *soto-gaijin*. They close ranks and work side by side as Japan Incorporated when the need arises.

We have heard businessmen and engineers in one country say that Toshiba is the technical leader. They win all the contracts. In an adjacent country they say Mitsubishi makes the best and best-priced of the same product. It puzzled us at first until the thought occurred to us that division of world markets has been settled in Tokyo.

This paradoxical balancing of the positive and negative forces of group mentality did not come about by chance. It was engineered, not in one grand plan of the powers meeting and fixing it, but in little steps, in their slow style of discussing alternatives for days on end, consulting everyone who is remotely concerned, and finally distilling a decision.

The picture is one of intermeshing of private and public sectors, closely knit groups, often fighting each other bitterly, as the warlords, the *daimyo*, fought and negotiated with each other in the past. It is groups of men with severe *samurai*-style self-discipline and determination to get out of the backward pits they believe they are in, respecting their masters but having a voice to say their piece. And respecting the feelings of their opponents, within or outside the group. Working in systems that understand human weaknesses, yet bogging themselves down with the intricacies of it all. Moving slowly but always in the right directions.

This is Japanese business, reflecting the Japanese personality.

Having stated this, one would expect individuals to be suppressed and few entrepreneurs to rise up in the business world. But the fact is that many of the giants in industry and trading have been built by outstanding individuals. In spite of the rigidity of their systems, men with drive and determination have broken through the traditional barriers and come out on top. There are ladders for the truly great on their snakes-and-ladders boards. These men were not thrust upwards by the system. They led and were the engines of growth of the empires they now control. Men like Matsushita Konosuke, Honda Soichiro, Akio Morita (Sony), Yoshida Tadao (Y.K.K.), Kazuma Tateishi (Tateishi Electric), Kauru Iue (Sanyo), Kazuo Inamori (Yashica), Takeshi Mitarai (Canon) ...

All this describes the system in Japan. What will your problems be? Perhaps the survey carried out by the Daiichi Kangyo Bank a few years ago may indicate the main problems.

A questionnaire sent to 300 foreign businessmen gave the following responses.

What is the most frustrating problem for you in doing business in Japan?
- Difficulty in expressing subtle nuances, 40%
- Japanese people tend to look at foreigners in a special way, 39.3%
- Difference in the way work progresses, 27%

What aspects of Japanese business do you find hard to understand?
- Many meetings never reach a final conclusion, 37.3%
- It takes a long time to reach a decision, 32.3%
- Too much importance is placed on title, 31.7%

It is time to deal with some aspects of the business world, giving a nutshell summary of each aspect.

The Zaibatsu

As one would expect, buddy-buddy and old school tie links would breed monopolies, with their positive and negative effects.

In Japan the *Zaibatsu*, a sort of clan of the giants, ruled the business world before the war. It was dismantled during the Occupation, but it never died. What is more important to appreciate, if your company is not in the league of the giants, is that the spirit of the *Zaibatsu* survives in principle.

The Sogo-shosa

These are the conglomerates which started off as trading companies. *Sogo* is general, *shosa* is trading. It would be better to translate *sogo* as 'anything under the sun'. They handle about 50% of all Japanese exports and about 60% of imports. Whatever field you are in, you will cross the path of a *sogo-shosa* one day.

There are six on top of the list. They watch each other's ranking by sales like racehorse breeders. But it really doesn't matter to the average businessman who's bigger than whom. The six who top the list are:

- C. Itoh & Co. Ltd
- Mitsui & Co. Ltd
- Sumitomo Corp.
- Marubeni Corp.
- Mitusbishi Corp.
- Nissho Iwai Corp.

From a business student's point of view, their strengths are interesting. Many of their strengths arise from their size.

- They deal with the world and can take the waves of economies of different countries by averaging it all out.
- They import and export and can balance foreign currency fluctuations to a large extent.
- They have financial muscle. Every *sogo-shosa* has its brother bank, which has a better knowledge of their export potential than any other bank has.
- They have a fantastic information network. In fact they have not fully exploited this – in spite of their computerisation of all the data – because of the volume and diversity of their input.

Some think that data banks now being built up by competitors in other parts of the world are eroding this advantage, but the whole spirit of collecting data and the reach of the tentacles of the *sogo-shosa* will probably keep them in front. It is really impressive how they are able to manage their massive organisations without, so far, showing signs of slipping, in the face of the scale of their operations.

If western morality had not created or accepted the sweatshops of the industrial revolution, nor stretched the powers of monopolies in the USA beyond the arbitrary limits society set, would the world not be a better place today? It is certainly a better place for the Japanese because of the *sogo-shosa*.

Here is one little aside on the *sogo-shosa* helping both buyers and sellers in a narrow slot of raw materials about ten years or more ago. Asbestos fibre: a dirty word today.

Russia had the raw material that could challenge the Canadian and South African holds on the market, at good prices. Many buyers went through the painful process of doing trial runs with the first delivery, finding the material suitable, and then being shocked at the variations of the second and third shipments. Not that the overall quality varied in absolute standard. It's just that machines using asbestos have to be adjusted to different characteristics of the raw material. Neither were the Russians trying to pull a fast one. They just could not organise what shipment came from which of their many mines.

One *sogo-shosa* saw an opportunity. They committed themselves to huge quantities out of Russia. Then they used their organisation to channel product from different mines to the right buyers.

It was not just a case of having the muscle. It was seeing the opportunity and having the organisation to exploit it.

Distribution and Wholesalers

The distribution system in Japan is unique and too complex to describe here. Just be aware that it is one of the most cumbersome systems in the world, where middlemen in layers take commission slices that bump up the factory to shop-shelf price differences, and that it is finally being eroded.

Financial Aspects

The auditing system is different from what you are used to – wherever you have come from. You may meet an officer known as the *kansayaku*, the Statutory Examiner, when you are introduced to all the officials. Exactly what he does is not certain.

The banking system is a little different, but is easy to understand. Finding finance is relatively easy.

Legal Aspects

This is totally different from British or Napoleonic law. You are advised to find out more about it.

The Labour Market

There are a few characteristics that should be noted.

First, the labour unions are organised on a company basis, and not on a trade or craft basis. Coupled with the lifetime employment system, this has weakened labour unions over the years. Union membership has dropped from a peak of 50% to under 26.8% in 1991. The company-based organisation of unions has probably been a major factor in getting unions to agree to a reduction of operators with new technologies, as agreements could be reached on staff redeployment within the company.

In recent years, unions have taken the long-range attitude that pushing up wage demands will eventually result in staff reduction. They have shifted their stand to shorter working hours.

One must appreciate that the unions do not have the political and social history of unions in Britain and many ex-colonies. For one thing, there is no class division in Japanese society similar to the proletariat-bourgeoise division. There are strata, but these do not impinge on the labour-management union stances.

Another unique feature of Japanese unions is the yearly 'spring offensive' when unions bargain for pay increments and additional benefits.

Some years ago I was alarmed during a visit to Japan to see what I thought was an aggressive demonstration of the unions with their protest banners in red, suggesting communist bitterness. I stood on the street and watched the demonstration. Then, to my surprise, the men, red-faced with the exertion of their shouting and waving placards, got into buses and began singing happily as the buses drove off, as though they were going home from a picnic.

I saw then that it was a ritual show of force that they had to display – like the ritualistic cooperation of buyers and sellers at the stock exchange on the first day of trading every year, pulling together to ensure that it is a bullish market. For good luck. For superstition's sake.

The bonus in Japan is not regarded as a merit payment as it is in the West. Bonus payments started with special payments to workers before their summer vacations and the New Year holidays. They are an expression of thanks from the company. The quantum varies with business conditions and the company's ability to pay. In a way, they are a form of profit sharing, but the option is in the employers' hands and the unions have no say in the bonus quantum.

Management of Firms

> "Japanese and American management is 95% the same and differs in all important aspects."
>
> —Fujisawa Takeo of Honda Motor Company

Here, let us try to cover the 'important aspects'.

"Open the door and here are the people ..."

Organisation charts of Japanese companies look more American than European. The big boss is the chairman, the *kaichoh*. (Note that *cho* is a longish sound.)

Under him are the president, *shachoh*, vice-presidents, *fuku shachoh*, managing director, *senmu torishimariyaku* (take it syllable by syllable), senior executive directors, *johmu torishimariyaku*, and directors, *torishimariyaku*. *Yaku* is a word used for officials.

These directors may have got there by sheer seniority. It is one of the norms of their system: seniority is of great importance. It takes really exceptional talent to jump the queue, but it does ensure that run-of-the-mill-high-flyers do not shoot up too fast. Be aware that on the average a Japanese company has about 10% outside directors.

The next level is the *buchoh*, the department manager, and under him is the deputy department manager, *buchoh dairi*. There may also be an assistant department manager, the *buchoh hosa*. The section manager is the *kachoh*; the supervisor, *kari kachoh*; and foremen, *hancho*.

You have to play it by ear when you meet all these people. In general, the chairman (*kaichoh*) would be a retired president (*shachoh*). The effective chief executive is the president. Vice-presidents (*fuku shachoh*) may be genuine assistants to the president, or nominal vice-presidents, retired nicely by the company to keep their egos cossetted and the president's job enhanced by a retinue of vice-presidents.

The *buchoh*, or the *kachoh*, managers of departments or sections, would probably be the key men to you.

Making decisions through **nemawashi** *and* **ringi**

Do not expect to study the men you meet and seek out the kingpin, then zone in on him and get a decision. You may be right in identifying him as the kingpin in the set-up. He may be completely in favour of your scheme. But he himself does not have the power to decide. He will have to manipulate it.

The decision-making system is a long, drawn-out process. There are basically two stages. The first is *nemawashi*.

Literally, *nemawashi* means to dig around the roots of a plant as a preliminary to transplanting. It is either a feeling out of the group's reaction to a proposal or a gentle forewarning of things to come, and preparation for acceptance. It is a device that allows probing without calling for opinions or reactions that may incur confrontation and loss of face.

You may have come across it at home. The marketing manager or the boss himself suddenly throws it out to you over a drink, "What do you think of Peter's idea on those widgets?" The difference is that the boss or the marketing manager at home will only sound you out if he's not sure of your reaction. In Japan it is *always* done. It does allow amendment of the idea to soften its impact.

The second round of kicking-it-around is the *ringi*. A *ringi-sho*, a circulating paper, is started. It may go round in the same level of the organisation chart, or it may go up or down. This is after the discussion, the *nemawashi*, stage. In a way, it tells one what has finally come out in the wash after digging around the roots. One is expected to put one's *hanko*, personal seal, which is equivalent to a signature, to the *ringi-sho*. It is an information shot: *This is what we are going to do. Speak now or forever hold your peace* – or, paraphrased into Japanese business words, *This is what is going to happen, and unless you want to lay your position in the company on the line, sign.*

This may sound terribly bureaucratic, but the effect of the *ringi-sho* is that once the boss-man has put his seal on it, action starts and it races through the organisation because there is no more briefing to do.

Today, there are some companies who are ditching these traditional systems and making go/no-go decisions at the table. You have to feel the situation out.

Lifetime Employment

Although the Japanese system may appear to be somewhat ideal, it has its drawbacks. One of these is carrying the deadwood, particularly the deadwood who have been promoted and exposed by the Peter Principle, which states that each employee is eventually promoted to a level of incompetence. The Japanese firm does not shoot them but puts them to pasture within the firm. They have a delightful term for them: the *madogiwa-zoku*, the tribe by the windows, because their desks are on the fringe of the office, next to the windows through which they alone have time to gaze. They often have nice titles, like manager or sub-manager, but no real responsibilities. In a way, the company is carrying a social burden.

The so-called lifetime employment terminates at 55, 57 or 60. This is the *teinen*, the age of stopping. The Japanese sometimes use the term *uchikirareru*, hit and cut off. The private sector gives a lump sum to retirees.

Apart from the many systems of operation, some of which have been described above, Japanese companies have many physical practices to keep the message of being one big family constantly alive. You may find that these remind you of your schooldays or of military regimentation. The *chorei* is an early morning assembly of all employees. There will be a pep talk, or singing of the *shaka*, the company song (any self-respecting company must have its own song, of course). The *shaze* or *shakun*, company motto or principles, will sometimes be repeated. All this may amuse you but the best attitude to show is that you find it all very interesting. Stifle any sign of ridicule.

Uniforms for office staff and factory staff are the general rule. You should try to live with this. Kicking against the system or changing it is going to cause more bewilderment than the satisfaction it may give you or your staff.

Office Arrangements

All offices are open-plan arrangements. Only the department head will have his own office. It has its merit of open communication to compensate for its lack of privacy. It suits the Japanese. One rarely talks to a man of another company across his desk. There are always many rooms for meetings, which provide the necessary privacy and keep the 'outsiders' out of the body of the office.

Meeting and Dealing with the Japanese

The social rules of meeting described under socialising with the Japanese in Chapter 5 apply to business meetings. So do the rules of card exchange and bowing. Seating protocol is also the standard of social intercourse. It would save all parties a lot of embarrassment if you knew that as a visitor you should sit on the seat furthest away from the door, and if you did not object to where they place you.

One surprise you will have at least once on your first visit, unless you've read about it, is that although you have arranged to meet Hara-san, there are three or four smiling faces bowing pleasantly to you. A one-to-one meeting is as rare as hen's teeth. It is part of the group-work system. This may appear to be a waste of executive manpower, but it extracts the most from a meeting. If you have come with your team, the practice is to line up the two teams facing each other. You do not break up their ranks by thrusting yourself in between on the host's side of the table.

A meeting will start off with pleasantries. To get down to the business at hand at once, even if a time pressure is hanging heavily over both parties, is just not done.

You will note that they are taking copious notes. This is partly because they aim to maximise the time spent at the meeting and partly because they are always hungry for data. Data is very important to them. You will please them if you have data on your home market, or what similar industries do, or anything remotely connected with the business, to hand out. It is another lesson to learn from the Japanese business style.

The language hurdle arises very often. You should bear in mind that individuals always have a gap between oral delivery of a foreign language and aural comprehension of it. A man who speaks fluently may have difficulty in understanding you. Or it could be vice versa for the introverted, shy person. Like people the world over, they may use the tricks of pretending not to understand, or asking for translations to get thinking time.

We have warned you earlier about the *Hai!* It doesn't always mean yes. It often means, *I understand what you have asked.*

Truths and Misconceptions

If you asked people who have done business with the Japanese what they are like, you would probably get a very mixed collection of angry, prejudiced answers like 'a bunch of crooks', spiels of glowing admiration, and a lot in between.

One can say this of any people in the world: that there are good guys and bad guys everywhere, and it's impossible to generalise. One can generalise about business styles in different countries although here, too, subjectivity cannot be eliminated.

With the Japanese being such a homogeneous people, and the government and the large companies exerting so much influence – working as Japan Inc., as some would say – Japan is probably one country about which one *can* make generalisations with a certain amount of confidence. Many businessmen do, but they are not always right. Some generalisations are discussed below.

The Japanese will squeeze the blood out of you.

Yes, they will, but not in blatant, unethical ways. Some of their business ethics are different from those of the West but most of it is a universally accepted norm. The Japanese will squeeze you at the negotiating table. They will throw in every trick, including the 'I don't understand what you are saying' one. They will play every card they hold to their advantage.

But once the deal is settled, they will honour their promises under the agreement. And they will do this on principle. There are two deep-seated reasons for this. First, they will not lose face by going back on their word, and second, as most business agreements involve working together to achieve something, you become part of the team when you get into bed with them.

I have a Canadian friend who now thinks they are not too bad to work with. However, on his first visit to Tokyo they met him almost as soon as he checked into the hotel when he arrived in the evening and took him out to dinner followed by an unforgettable night of carousing at some Ginza bar. He woke up the next morning feeling terrible, but being a man of diverse strengths he knew that his hosts would be feeling twice as bad. To his horror, every face at the negotiating table was a new face, fresh and smiling after a quiet night at home.

Perhaps stories like his have given rise to their reputation for dirty tactics. Was that a dirty tactic? Not quite cricket?

They can take initial losses and will drag you into terrible cash-flow problems.

True in a way. Their whole attitude to business is long-term. Everyone is committed to the company for life. The directors are not watching the annual or six-month bottom line as they do in the West. This is their strength. Their banks know this, unlike banks elsewhere.

You must never forget this premise and the way they always look at the longer term, and that their stamina enables them to operate towards longer-term goals.

You can never get a decision from them.

A half-truth, as you will realise from their consensus approach to making decisions. But when a decision is reached they do not go back on it.

They get themselves twisted into knots with their hierarchal system.

Often. I have had the experience of working with a large Japanese company to make a presentation to a potential customer. I insisted on a dry run before the big day, during which I discovered that the number one man who was going to lead was terrible, not just in his Japlish. Number two was very good. I suggested that number one just say a few nice words and leave it to number two. To them it was inconceivable I should even have suggested it!

They will take your technology and that's the end of it.
They will. It is a fine line of commercial morality. What if they manufacture your design in a more efficient way than you do at home? What if they take off from the base technology you provided?

Technology transfer agreements cannot cover all the possibilities. Only genuine cooperation can take advantage of the Japanese strength in group thinking that sometimes throws out the lateral jump.

Here is an anecdote about stealing technology. An Australian company on the cutting edge of a very specialised technology started talks with a large Japanese firm on technology transfer and joint operations. Teams visited each other's factories in Australia and Japan. The deal did not go through, mainly because of market considerations.

One year after it fell apart the Australian company was surprised to receive a bank draft from the Japanese with a note. It said that while they were visiting one of the factories in Australia, they saw a unique method of handling the product from factory to yard. It was not a thing of clever engineering. It was one of those why-did-I-not-think-of-it devices. They copied it. The cheque covered what they estimated would be a just payment for the idea.

The Japanese are the world's worst salesmen.
They are. They hardly ever go out to sell in a one-to-one talking attack. In Japan the purchasing officer who's going to make the decision there and then is a rare bird. It's a waste of time and effort to do the hard-sell act. Their very culture inhibits them from imposing their will forcibly on another.

But they are the world's best marketing people. They can sit down in Tokyo and plan the approach and selling strategy into any market in the world because of their use of many minds working together.

Selling is a one-person task. Marketing is a team task. This is a good example of the strength and weakness of their group psyche. Would the best combination be a Japanese marketing team, away from it all in Tokyo with an American-Irish-Lebanese-Chinese-Indian sale force?

Your company sets up a thriving joint-venture with a Japanese company. Then you leave your company and work for another. They don't want to know you then. Neither do the customers with whom you developed such good relationships.

Partly true. It's very much a case of individuals. But you can be sure that if you go to them with a competitive product, they will bow you out of the room.

The question is one of personal relationships versus company relationships. It does not just depend on the individual. The particular Japanese company's attitude counts.

I had an interesting personal experience when I was an employee of a big company. I sat down with the prospective customer, a German supplier and the main Japanese bidder to discuss a large supply and install a contract of specialised and complicated mechanical equipment for about ten hectic days, talking with them to the prospective buyer all day, then sitting down over the evening meal with the Japanese and analysing the day's discussions.

We got the job.

I left the company I was working for soon after the project started. Three years later, I was in a completely different business, and a nobody in that field. A phone call came through to me. It was the Japanese company.

"The project is completed. The opening ceremony is next month. We would like you to be there since you were present at its birth."

What other company would do that?

The heavyweights have got it all fixed. Don't try.

Maybe. There is no doubt that the heavyweights use their power to the hilt.

One of the heavyweights had a factory in Singapore. A smaller, but formidable competitor in Japan began exploring the possibilities of setting up in Singapore. A friend of mine helped them. The heavyweight corporation rang him and in their indirect way suggested that the competitor in Japan was really doing the wrong thing. After all, they had never operated outside Japan. He would save them from making a huge mistake if he could persuade them to drop the crazy thought. Pull and push was exerted on my friend to dissuade them from coming to Singapore. He ignored the call.

The competitor company rang him three months later to say they had decided not to set up in Singapore. There is no doubt about it: the Japanese use their muscle when they have it. Or their weight – like *sumo* wrestlers.

If you're trying to manage a Japanese outfit in Japan, it's almost impossible to spot personal conflicts early.
Very true. The exterior mask they put on is very difficult for a *gaijin* to penetrate. You will not be able to see personalities clashing until you live in Japan for a long time. You have to rely on your number two, assuming he's Japanese, of course.

If there is tension developing, perhaps the best rallying point is the company – for the greater good of the company, rather than your personal charisma. The scene is different there.

They cannot see the trees for the wood. They cannot see that our Head Office has its faults.
Yes, in that context. If you represent your company in a joint operation with a Japanese company, your outright criticism of one department in your Head Office will cast doubt on your integrity. The Japanese do not knock family in the presence of others. If you know that the shipping department back at the ivory tower at home has always been manned by nincompoops, keep it to yourself and find some plausible explanation for the blunder. Never forget you represent the whole company, like an ambassador.

The Japanese are 'D' people; not 'R' for basic research people.
It is an interesting question. But in business, development matters more than research in the long term, doesn't it?

The main message of this chapter is that it is a very different business world. There's a lot to learn about dealing with the Japanese; and a lot to learn from them.

— *Chapter Nine* —

RESOURCES

An Annotated Bibliography

Listed below are some books with brief generalisations on them, except for some in the business book list. The selection and comments are naturally subjective.

The best way to use this list is to go to bookshops and libraries and flip through the books available. Then look up the list below to see if there are comments which will help you in your buy-or-borrow decision.

GENERAL

Cultures of the World, Japan. One of the Times Editions Singapore series, by Rex Shelley, 1990. Well illustrated, sweeping across the whole panorama of Japan, the Japanese and their culture and customs. A quick introduction to Japan, easily read.

Instant Japanese. Masahiro Watanabe and Kei Nagashima, Yohan Publications Inc, Japan. A quickie book to buy if you do not intend to learn the language. You will always need some phrase book to survive; this one gives you a little more than the ordinary tourist's phrase book.

THE JAPANESE

Japanese Society. Chie Nakane, first published in 1970, now available in Penguin Books Ltd, UK edition. An in-depth study of the Japanese, which examines their group structures and psychology. Has to be read with concentration, but recommended for anyone who really wants to understand the Japanese.

Land of the Rising Yen. George Mikes, 1970, Andre Deutsch, UK. A good first introduction book to read lying by the poolside or in bed, chuckling at the author's experiences and comments.

The Adventures of An Expat in Tokyo. Robert J. Collins, 1987, Charles E. Tuttle Company Inc., Vermont, USA. A very entertaining book from which one learns quite a lot about the Japanese through the eyes of Max Danger, a character the author first created in a series of articles in the *Tokyo Weekender*, a weekly English language paper.

The Chrysanthemum and the Sword. Ruth Benedict, first published 1946, 42nd printing by Charles E. Tuttle Company, 1987. A classic study of the Japanese by an anthropologist. Rather serious, but interesting reading. The author started studying the Japanese during World War II, without going to Japan.

The Japanese. E.O. Reischauer, 1979, Harvard University Press. Generally accepted as one of the best books on the Japanese, by a man who knew them well. He was once the United States ambassador to Japan. Perhaps outdated in parts.

The Japanese. Jack Seward, 10th edition 1982, Lotus Press, Tokyo, Japan. Seward covers all the important aspects of the Japanese writing in a style of his own, and provides plenty of statistics. He has a good food chapter and notes on topics like humour, their sex life, their views of *gaijin* and the *konketsuji*, the mixed Caucasian-Japanese bloods, which most similar books do not discuss.

The Japanese Mind. Robert C. Christopher, Pan Books, UK, 1984. Although the title may give one an impression of a dead serious book probing the cybernetics and psychology of the Japanese mind, it is written in the journalistic style of the author's experience, with many human anecdotes. It deals with the main points which baffle westerners and, though written nearly nine years ago, focuses on many perennial characteristics of the Japanese psyche.

The Japanese Today, Change and Continuity. E.O. Reischauer, Belknap Press of Harvard University Press, 1988.

Your Life in Tokyo, A Manual for Foreign Residents. The Japan Times, 1987.

HISTORY

A History of Modern Japan. Richard Storry, 1960, Penguin Books Limited, UK. The best brief history of Japan from the 16th century to the 1960s, with a summary of the preceding centuries. There are also some interesting comments on the Japanese character in it.

Travellers' Tales of Old Japan. Compiled by Michael Wise, 1985, Times Books International. A collection of sketches of old Japan from 1854 to 1923. A book to keep on your bedside table to read a chapter every night, for amusement and for learning a little about old Japan and the Japanese.

Unbeaten Tracks in Japan. Isabella L. Bird. A 19th century travel journal which includes the aborigines of Yezo, the Shrine of Nikko, etc.

FOOD

Eating in Japan. Japan Travel Bureau, 5th edition 1988. This pocket-sized booklet is the best quick introduction to Japanese food. It not only tells you about the different kinds of food but also gives information on ingredients, utensils and local specialities, and is the only book we have seen which gives a map of the different varieties of *miso* across Japan.

Japanese Cookery. Jon Spayde, Quarto Publishing Limited, UK, 1984. A beautifully illustrated book. Books like these should be looked at even if you don't want to cook Japanese food. Knowing what the ingredients are, how a dish is cooked and what it looks like makes it so much easier to order. If you live in London and want to try Japanese food before you go to Japan, there is a list of Japanese restaurants in London in the book.

BUSINESS

Business Otsukiai. A Guide to Japanese Business Protocol, translated and edited by James V. Reilly, 1991, NTT Mediascope, Tokyo. Easy to read book with drawings, some quite humorous. A lot of it is not particularly Japanese but general business protocol. Yet even the un-Japanese parts on management and sales are worth reading as a refresher.

Words Mean Business. Mitsubishi Corporation, edited by Rex Shelley, 1984, Times Books International, Singapore. The book explains the meaning of words used in Japanese business. It gives one a quick picture of the Japanese businessman, and to a large extent the Japanese character. In Japanese and English, it also tells the Japanese what is being said about their systems and about them as businessmen.

Listed below without comments are books on business to help the man or woman who feels lost in the Japanese corporate jungle.

Corporate Strategies in Japan. K. Odaka, R. Grondine, S. Mizushima, 1985, Longman.

Doing Business in Japan. JETRO, 1984, Gakuseisha Publishing Co. Ltd.

Introducing Japanese Companies. Satoshi Sugita, The Japan Times.

Introduction to Japanese Law. Yosiyuki Noda, translated and edited by Anthony H. Angelo, 1976, University of Tokyo Press.

Japan As Number One. Ezra Vogel, 1979, Harvard University Press.

Japan Today. W.H. Forbes, 1975, Harper and Row.

Japanese Business Pioneers. Dr Kazuyoshi Kamioka, 1988, Heian International Inc., California, USA.

Kaisha, The Japanese Corporation. James C. Abegglen, 1986, Harper and Row.

The Art of Japanese Management. R. Pasquale and A. Athos, 1981, Penguin.

The Book of Five Rings: The Real Art of Japanese Management. Miyamoto Musashi, 1982, Bantam Books Inc.

The Japanese Company. Rodney Clark, 1979, Yale University Press.

The Japanese Economy, What Makes It Tick. Isamu Miyazaki, Chairman, Daiwa Institute of Research, translated by Simul International, 1990, Simul Press, Tokyo.

LEARNING THE JAPANESE LANGUAGE

A Guide to Reading and Writing Japanese. Charles E. Tuttle Co. Inc., 1st edition 1959, 25th printing 1973. An essential book for *kanji* learners. The strokes are very clearly shown. The greatest merit of the book is that it is based on the Japanese Ministry of Education syllabuses and takes one through the same graduated steps Japanese schoolchildren go through. It teaches 1,850 characters.

Beginner's Dictionary of Chinese-Japanese Characters. Arthur Rose-Innes, Dover Publications Inc., USA. Not for the beginner, but quite necessary for one who is about halfway through the Tuttle book described above. There is no other dictionary as easy to use as this for the English-speaking intermediate student.

This dictionary includes many phrases with each character, unlike Tuttle's *Guide* above and *Essential Kanji* (see below) which give two to four phrases in which the character is used. One of the frustrating things about the first stages of learning *kanji* is that you look up a character in the simpler books, then find that only a few phrases which use the character are given. You have to go to the Japanese-English dictionary to get the exact meaning of a two-character phrase you are looking for. The Rose-Innes dictionary, however, does not have an index to trace a character by its sound as Tuttle's *Guide* and *Essential Kanji* do.

Brush Up Your Japanese. Oreste and Elisa Enko Vaccari, 1969, Gakujutsu Seihan Company, Tokyo. A curious book containing a mixed collection of translations in 52 short lessons, lists of ono matopoeia and Japanese names. A good supplementary textbook, but not a main learner's textbook, for the intermediate student. Some of the translations are from the newspapers. It seems to stop suddenly.

Essential Kanji. P.G. O'Neill, Professor of Japanese at the School of Oriental and African Studies, London, 1st edition 1973, 12th printing 1986, John Weatherhill Inc, USA. Very similar to Tuttle's *Guide* described above, but much better laid out with a little more information on each character. It has 2000 characters, 150 more than the other book.

Kenkyusha's New School Japanese-English dictionary. Just one sample of the many dictionaries available. If you are a serious student make sure the dictionary you buy has the *kanji*. When buying a Japanese-English dictionary you can either get one arranged in the western alphabetic order or in the Japanese A-I-U-E-O, KA-KI-KU-KE-KO order, but note that it will take you some time to get used to the Japanese system.

Read Japanese Today. Ken Walsh, first published 1979, Charles E. Tuttle Company Inc., Vermont, USA. Even if you do not intend to study Japanese seriously, this book is worth reading as it shows how the written characters were derived. And as the title claims, it does give one an immediate ability to read some common characters. It is easy to read.

Shogyo Shokai no Eigo. Satoshi Sugita, 1985, The Japan Times. This book has not got an English title but it is a very good book for intermediate students of the language who are in business. It deals with different aspects of the Japanese business world in both Japanese and English.

Teach Yourself Japanese. Probably the best book for getting started. It does not, however, teach the Japanese scripts.

THE ARTS

A History of Japanese Literature. W.G. Aston, first published 1899, 1972 edition by Charles E. Tuttle Company Inc., Vermont, USA. A big book, 402 pages, with many extracts from translations of the classical works. If you are interested in Japanese literature, read this after Donald Keene's 110-page introduction, to refresh your memory and flesh in parts which Keene has skimmed over. The 1972 edition does not update the book contents, and 'recent poetry' in the last chapter is poetry of the 1890s.

Form, Style, Tradition. Shuichi Kato, translated by John Bester, 1971, University of California Press. The subtitle, 'Reflections on Japanese Art and Society', describes the book, which discusses the interplay between life and the arts. One needs some knowledge of the Japanese arts to appreciate it fully. It is a thought-provoking book.

Haiku. R.H. Blyth, first printed 1950, The Hokuseido Press, Tokyo, in four volumes: *Culture*, *Spring*, *Summer-Autumn*, *Autumn-Winter*. Four beautiful books, a big investment, in English, with the Japanese texts, discussion, references to Chinese poetry that influenced the Japanese, with the old Chinese texts, and some nice reproductions of Japanese paintings. Each book is subdivided into subject areas such as The Season, Fields and Mountains, and Gods and Buddhas.

Japanese Literature. Donald Keene, 1955, Charles E. Tuttle Company Inc., Vermont, USA, subtitled 'an introduction for western readers'. A good introduction by Donald Keene, who has written many books on Japan and the Japanese.

Japanese Theatre. Faubian Bowers, first published 1952, republished by Charles E. Tuttle Company Inc., Vermont, USA. A good book for one really interested, but too serious for an introduction. Well illustrated. Mr Bowers was helped by Japanese scholars and his personal acquaintance with many Japanese actors.

Modern Japanese Poetry. Translated and compiled by Edith Marcombe Shiffert and Yuki Sawa, 1972, Charles E. Tuttle Company Inc., Vermont, USA. Worth reading, although the youngest poets translated were born in 1931. It is generally poetry of the first half of the 20th century, influenced by T.S. Eliot, Whitman, Valery, Pound, Cocteau, Breton, Eluard, Aragon, and other French and English poets. It includes works of Sakutaro Hagiwara, then thought to be the foremost of the modern Japanese poets. The introduction reviews English publications of modern Japanese poetry up to the early 1970s, and discusses the problems of translating poetry.

The first translation is a poem titled, 'A man sharpening a knife'. It starts with 'Somewhere a knife is being sharpened./Though the sun is already sinking, it is still being sharpened ...'

Some Japanese Portraits. Donald Keene, 1st edition 1978, Kodansha International/USA Ltd. Supplementary reading for one who has read about Japanese literature. It is a collection of essays and translations of Japanese writing in prose and verse from the 15th to the 19th century. Yet it is a book anyone can dip into and enjoy if one is not too concerned with trying to see the material in it against the total background of Japanese literature.

The Dawns of Tradition. Edited by Teiji Itoh, President, Kogakuin University, and Gregory Clark, Professor, Sophia University, 1983, published by the Nissan Motor Company Ltd. A beautiful book sweeping across many areas of the visual arts, beautifully illustrated in full colour, including arts like sword making, lacquer, bonsai, clothing. A book one would want to keep, but perhaps not easily found in bookshops today.

The Ogura Anthology of Japanese Waka. Haruo Miyata, 1981, Osaka Kyoiku Tosho Co. Ltd. A translation of the famous Hyakknin-Isshu, a hundred poems by a hundred poets. Good, but translated into 19th century style poetical English.

The Penguin Book of Japanese Verse. Translated with an introduction by Geoffery Bownas and Anthony Thwaite, first published 1964. The best readily available collection of all forms of Japanese verse. The 84-page introduction is excellent. It has a few of the humorous *senryo* poems which most serious books on Japanese verse omit.

The Translations of Ezra Pound. 1954, Faber and Faber, UK. The 147 pages on the *noh* plays are wonderful reading for anyone interested in *noh*. Ezra Pound has captured the spirit of the original. It is not just translations but there are notes on Fenollosa, comparisons with western theatre, costumes, etc.

TRAVELLING IN JAPAN

A Haiku Journey. Translated and introduced by Dorothy Britton, photographs by Dennis Stock, 1984, 1st edition 1974, revised 1980, Kodansha International Ltd. A delightful book which is the translation of parts of the poet Matsuo Basho's journal of his famous tour on Honshu in 1689. The original, in old Japanese, is also given, and will be of much interest to students of the language.

Although it is the translation of a 400-year-old book, this book and Lesley Downer's *On the Narrow Road to the Deep North* (see below) are easily readable entertainments from which one learns something more about the Japanese.

Festivals of Japan. A pocket book of the Japan Travel Bureau series, which will keep you awake for half the night when you bring it home. The fascinating festivals of Japan in 191 small pages that will stir you to plan your next vacation, as will the whole series, the best starter's booklets.

Fodor's Japan. Fodor's Travel Publications Inc. An excellent book with plenty of information on the country and its restaurants, history, festivals, museums and sports. A good book to browse through as an introduction to Japan.

Gateway to Japan. June Kinoshita and Nicholas Palevsky, 1989, Kodansha International. A general guide to Japan, packed with useful information for the traveller. Generally similar to Fodor's guide.

Insight Guides, Japan. 1992, APA Publications (HK) Ltd. A general guide book with beautiful colour photographs. It is a heavy book but the print is easy to read. However, it does not have all the detail that Fodor's and the Gateway books above have. (There's at least one mistake. The height of Mount Fuji has been shortened by a thousand metres.)

Japan, The New Official Guide. Edited with the cooperation of the Japan National Tourist Organisation, JTB Inc., 1991. An excellent guide.

Japanese Festivals. Helen Bauer and Sherwin Carlquist, 1965, Charles E. Tuttle Company Inc., Vermont, USA. This book describes 355 festivals, giving the story behind their origins. The Japan Travel Bureau booklet and most guide books give information on Japanese festivals, but it is usually sketchy. You'll get much more detail in this book.

Japanese Castles. Michio Fujioka, translated by Don Kenny, 12th edition 1986, Hoikusha Publishing Co. Ltd, Japan. If castles are your beat, this is your pocket-size booklet. Beautifully illustrated, it explains some of the castle designs. You may find that you have to keep looking back and forward to get your teeth into Japanese castles, but it is still worth buying.

Japanese Pilgrimage. Oliver Statler, 1984, Pan Books Ltd. A fascinating traveller's story of a pilgrimage encircling the saint Kobo Daishi's home island. Don't be put off by the title; it's not a religious book, although there is plenty on religion. It is full of details of Japanese behaviour and their life.

Kogakko shakai ryochi zucho. Primary school book of maps of resources, Teikoku Book House. The primary schoolchildren's map book, cheap, all in Japanese, with the *kanji* pronunciations in *hiragana*, and with information on the natural resources, industrial production, and historic and scenic sites.

On the Narrow Road to the Deep North. Lesley Downer, 1989, Jonathan Cape, UK. A book that anyone interested in the Japanese *haiku* poet Matsuo Basho will find most interesting, as it records the author's travels along the route taken by the poet 400 years earlier.

It gives a glimpse into rural Japanese life at the end of the 1980s; it will surprise you how many little pockets of the old ways still exist in Japan.

MISCELLANEOUS

Crossroads of Humour. Satoshi Sugita, 1981, Asahi Evening News. An interesting and curious book. In both English and Japanese and therefore of interest to the student of the Japanese language. It gives one an insight into Japanese humour. You will shake your head with either amazement or puzzlement at two-thirds of the jokes, and enjoy the other one-third.

Diplomatic Blue Book. Foreign Press Centre of Japan. The title is what it is all about. The Foreign Press Centre has other publications that may be of interest to you.

Discover Japan. By many contributors, and edited by Donald Richie; a re-publication in 1982 of the 1975 version is titled *A Hundred Things Japanese*. A 1987 edition, in two volumes, is available.

Kodansha International. A reference book giving one a kaleidoscopic picture of Japan, if you want to read it through. The average length of an item is one and a half pages. Every item is illustrated in some way or other. Donald Richie has written many books on Japan.

Japan Almanac. Boye De Mente, 1987, Passport Books, Illinois, USA. This is an alphabetically arranged reference book, like an illustrated dictionary but with one-paragraph to one-page explanations, covering most things you would like to look up, from the abacus to Zen food, including down-to-earth items like quality control and common signs one sees on the street and in shopping centres.

Japanese Etiquette. World Fellowship Committee of the Young Women's Christian Association of Tokyo, 1955, Charles E. Tuttle Company Inc., Vermont, USA. Most of the contents are outdated but it does show one how rigid Japanese etiquette was 40 years ago, and that what westerners today consider to be terribly formal is not half what it used to be before.

Japanese Paper Making. Timothy Barret, 1st edition 1983, John Weatherhill, USA. Not a book for the general reader, but an excellent book for one interested in Japanese *washi*, handmade paper. It goes into a lot of technical detail but is written in an easy style with anecdotes of the writer's conversations with some of the last of the old paper-making farmers and others. The introduction, 'Japanese Paper: Past and Present' is very good. We drew a lot of our notes on paper from it.

Lafcadio Hearn Series:

A Japanese Miscellany
Kotto: Being Japanese – Curios with Sundry Cobwebs
In Ghostly Japan
Kokoro: Hints and Echoes of Japanese Inner Life
Shadowings
Kwaidan: Stories and Studies of Strange Things

The Romance of the Milky Way

All by Lafcadio Hearn and published by Charles E. Tuttle Company Inc., Vermont, USA. Lafcadio Hearn has written a series of books over a very wide range of subjects, from insects to Japanese folk tales. Of Greek and Irish parentage, he started life as a journalist in America and came to Japan where, at the age of 41, he married the daughter of a *samurai* family and became a Japanese national. These are books for the person who likes to pick up curios and gets pleasure in scrutinising them carefully, but there are also parts of many of his books that make easy and fascinating reading.

Reading Your Way Around Japan – A Sign for Everyone. Boye De Menthe, Passport Books, Illinois, USA. It seems that there are more signs in Japan than in any other country in the world, and this book helps one learn the minimum Japanese to read the most common signs.

Sexy Laughing Stories of Old Japan. Adapted and translated by A. Dykstra, 1974, Japan Publications Inc., San Francisco, USA. The reason I have this book is that a friend who bought it wanted to throw it away. It is a strange collection of jokes. You will probably be amused by about 20% of them.

Space and Illusion in the Japanese Garden. Teiji Itoh, translated and adapted by Ralph Friedrich and Masajiro Shimamura, originally published in Japanese in 1965, Weatherhill Inc. 1980. Mostly in black and white, with 103 illustrations, it is recommended for anyone interested in landscaping gardens. The book deals with two Japanese concepts, the *shakkei*, literally ‘borrowed scenery’, and ‘the great within the small’.

English Language Newspapers available in Japan

Asahi Evening News

Daily Yomiuri

The Japan Times, which also has a weekly airmail edition

Mainichi Daily News

Telephones

Dial 110 for the police; 119 for fire or ambulance.

Red, Yellow and Green phones take 100 yen coins and/or phone cards. You can access 104 and 105 for directory assistance and 106 for collect calls, and you can reach the 100 operator, through whom you can get the call cost and make international calls.

Green phones are card-phones. Phone cards with stored value of 500 yen (US$4.70) and 1,000 yen (US$9.50) are sold at NTT offices or from machines.

Phone Numbers, Addresses of Organisations

Agape House, 5-4-37 Oizumi-machi, Nerima-ku, Tokyo 178-0062, Tel: (03) 3978-7878.

Central Metropolitan Police Board, Tel: (03) 3581-4321.

Economic Planning Agency, 3-1-1 Kasumigaseki, Chiyoda-ku, Tokyo 100-0013, Tel: (03) 3581-0261. Publications: *Annual Report on National Life*; *Economic Outlook Japan*; *Outlook and Basic Policy for the National Economy*. Sales agent: Government Publications Service Centre.

Government Publications Service Centre, 1-2 Kasumigaseki, Chiyoda-ku, Tokyo 100-0013, Tel: (03) 3504-3885.

Japan Economic Journal, Nihon Keizai Shimbun Sha, 1-9-5 Otemachi, Chiyoda-ku, Tokyo 100-0004, Tel: (03) 3270-0251.

Japan Guide Association, Shin-Kokusai Building, 4-1 Marunouchi 3-chome, Chiyoda-ku, Tokyo 100-0005, Tel: (03) 3213-2706.

Japan Helpline, Tel: toll-free, 24 hours (0120) 461-997.

Japan National Tourist Organisation, Headquarters: Kotsukaikan 10F, 10-1 Yurakucho 2-chome, Chiyoda-ku, Tokyo 100-0006, Tel: (03) 3216-1901.

Japan Travel Phone (9 a.m. to 5 p.m. every day). Outside Tokyo or Kyoto, Tel: toll-free (0088) 22-4800. In Tokyo, Tel: (03) 3201-2911, paying 10 yen per 3 minutes; in Kyoto, Tel: (075) 371-5649, paying the same rate.

Japan Yellow Pages, Ltd, English version, ST Building, 4-6-9

Iidabashi, Chiyoda-ku, Tokyo 102-0072, Tel: (03) 3239-3501, Fax: (03) 3237-8945.

Japanese Language School, Association of International Education, Japan, 4-5-29 Komaba, Meguru-ku, Tokyo 153, Tel: (03) 3467-3521.

ISS (Interlanguage Service Systems), Nihon Seimei Ichibancho Building, 7F, 23-3 Ichibancho, Chiyoda-ku, Tokyo 102-0082. Tel: 03-3230-4391.

JATA (Japan Association of Travel Agents), Zen Nittsu Kasumigaseki Building, 3-3 Kasumigaseki 3-chome, Chiyoda-ku, Tokyo 100-0013, Tel: (03) 3592-1271, Fax: (03) 3592-1268.

JR East Infoline (English), Tel: (03) 3423-0111.

Oak Associates (International Human Resource Services), Riviera 3B, 21-22 Higashiyama 1-chome, Meguro-ku, Tokyo 153, Tel: (03) 3760-8451, Fax: (03) 3760-8411.

Oak Associates (Welcome Furoshiki), Tel: (03) 5472-7077.

Teletourist (available 24 hours daily throughout the year), Tokyo, in English, Tel: (03) 3503-2911, Tokyo, in French, Tel: (03) 3503-2926. In and around Kyoto, in English, Tel: (075) 361-2911.

TELL (Tokyo English Life Line), Tel: (03) 3968-4099.

The Salvation Army, 2-17 Kanda Jimbocho, Chiyoda-ku, Tokyo 101-0051, Tel: (03) 3237-0881.

Tokyo Domestic Service Centre, 17-65-406 Akasaka 2-chome, Minato-ku, Tokyo 107-0052, Tel: (03) 3584-4760 or (03) 3584-4769.

Tourist Information Centre, Tokyo Kokusai Forum Building B1, 3-5-1 Marunochi, Chiyoda-ku, Tokyo 100-0005, Tel: (03) 3201-3331.

Hospitals

These hospitals in Tokyo have English-speaking doctors:

Hibiya Clinic, B1, Hibiya Mitsui Building, 1-2 Yurakucho 1-chome, Chiyoda-ku, Tokyo 100-0006 , Tel. (03) 3502-2681.

International Catholic Hospital, 5-1 Naka Ochiai 2-chome, Shinjuku-ku, Tokyo 161-0032, Tel. (03) 3951-1111.

St Luke's Hospital and Clinic, 9-1 Akashi-cho, Chuo-ku, Tokyo 104-0044, Tel: (03) 3541-5151.

Tokyo Medical and Surgical Clinic, No.32 Mori Building, 4-30 Shibakoen 3-chome, Minato-ku, Tokyo 105-0011, Tel: (03) 3436-3028.

In Yokohama: International Goodwill Hospital, 28-1, Nishigaoka 1-chome, Izumi-ku, Yokohama 245-0006, Tel: (045) 813-0221.

In Kyoto: Japan Baptist Hospital, 47 Yamamoto-cho, Kitashirakawa, Kyoto 606-8273, Tel: (075) 781-5191.

In Osaka: Yodogawa Christian Hospital, 2-9-26 Awaji, Higashi Yodogawa-ku, Osaka 533-0032, Tel: (06) 6322-2250.

International Time

Japan has only one time zone and no summer time changes. Japan time is 8 hours ahead of Greenwich Mean Time.

Public Holidays in Japan

January 1	New Year's Day
January 15	Coming of Age Day
February 11	National Foundation Day
March 21	Vernal Equinox
April 29	Greenery Day
May 3	Constitution Memorial Day
May 4	People's Holiday
May 5	Children's Day
September 15	Respect for the Aged Day
September 23	Autumnal Equinox
October 10	Health-Sports Day
November 3	Culture Day
November 23	Labour Thanksgiving Day

Signs

Four of the simpler *kanji* signs you should learn are:

- *Iriguchi*, entrance (入口, same as the Chinese, *jukuo*, entry mouth)
- *Deguchi*, exit (出口 , *chukuo*)
- *Onna*, women – toilets (女 , *nu*)
- *Otoko*, men – toilets (男 , *nan*)

Post Office

General Post Offices in the major cities are located near the central railway stations.

Measures

Japan is on the metric system.

Voltage is 100 volts AC, but cycles (Hertz) are different in western and eastern Japan. Tokyo is on fifty cycles.

Electricity in Japan is expensive. Relative costs of residential electricity on 1 January 1990 were:

3.6 times the cost in Quebec
2.35 times the cost in Australia
2.0 times the cost in Boston
1.7 times the cost in England and Wales

Lost and Found

The Japanese are very honest and if you have lost something it is worth checking to see if has been picked up.

The railways, *chikatetsu*, buses and taxis all have lost-and-found offices. After three days all items go to the Central Metropolitan Police Board. Tel: (03) 3581-4321.

Banks

Banks are open from 9 a.m. to 3 p.m. They are closed on Saturdays and Sundays and public holidays.

The National Flag

The national flag, known as *nisshoki*, the flag of the rising sun, is a simple red ball on a white background. It was first used on banners and shrine flags and in the 16th century to identify Japanese ships. It was adopted as the national flag in 1870.

A flag you may have seen, similar to the *nisshoki*, has red rays spreading out from the red sun core. That is the navy's flag.

The National Anthem of Japan

Kimi ga yo wa
Chiyo ni yachiyo ni
Sazare-ishi no iwao to narite
Koke no musu made.

May the sovereign reign,
For a thousand years, eight thousand years,
Till the little pebbles become rocks,
Covered with moss.
(Author's translation)

— *Chapter Ten* —

CULTURAL QUIZ

Try this ten-question quiz to test your new-found knowledge of the Japanese.

The quiz questions also contain some items for revision and one or two new points. Names used in the situations are purely fictitious.

SITUATION 1

Some years ago you decided that it's stupid to punish one's body with alcohol. There are so many pleasures of drinking one can enjoy without imbibing alcohol.

After your second day at the new place you are asked to join the other executives at the *akachochin*.

You agree. The music is so loud that no one hears you say you don't drink and a little wine-cup of *sake* is poured out for you. It's pretty dark, too, in the bar. The boss raises his cup to you with a lusty shout of "*Kanpai!*"

What should you do?

A Speak up loudly above the noise that you don't drink alcohol.
B Force yourself to knock it back. After all, it's not as if the doctor told you to lay off.
C Raise your cup in return, put it to your lips and put the cup down without drinking a sip.
D There's a table behind you that has not been cleared although the people who were around it have left. Since it's pretty dark, you lean over and tip the *sake* into a dirty glass.

Comments

A would be the honest, straightforward thing to do. But it would throw a damper on the party even before it starts.

B would be a mistake. You'll only postpone the problem to the next round, unless you want to sacrifice yourself for the evening.

C would be acceptable. You should explain later that you do not drink alcohol. There may be ribbing or guffaws, but you will probably have encountered that before. If you want to end it, tell them about the girl you met who quoted Percy Bysshe Shelley at you: "Lips that touch liquor shall not touch mine." And say you finally married her.

D, like *B*, is postponing the problem.

SITUATION 2

The scene: your living room. You have invited Kori-san, who you have come to know so well, and his wife, with Jimmy of IBM and Robert E. Brown, whom you've just met at the club, and their wives.

Kori-san brings a gift and presents it to you as he walks in when the rest of the party has already settled down. Your wife puts on her standard first act of being surprised and opens it at once, then does her second act of feigned delight at the little vase. It's nothing special.

Both Mr and Mrs Kori are terribly embarrassed.

Why?

A They are not used to your wife's gushing praises about the stupid little vase.

B She shouldn't have opened the present at once.

C She just ripped open the beautiful wrapping without a glance at it.

D They are just embarrassed to be the last guests to arrive.

Comments

A is a possibility. The Japanese avoid displays of emotion as far as possible.

B is most probably the real reason. The Japanese never open a gift in front of the giver. Perhaps it's just in case one shows on one's face that one's got three of them widgets already.

C may be a small cause of their feelings of discomfort. The wrapping is as important as the gift to the Japanese. It is part of their whole attitude to life. The sizzle is just as important as the steak.

D is unlikely. But they may be embarrassed if they were the first to arrive, and Kori-san will take a furtive glance at his watch to check if they haven't violated protocol by arriving before time, probably cursing himself for allowing so much time for possible traffic snarls.

SITUATION 3

Young Aoi Sudeo at the office is getting married. You've talked to Tsuji-san and he's told you what to do and you've got it pat this time. Not like that day when you walked into Uno-san's house with your shoes on shortly after you arrived. Tsuji-san has even arranged to pick you and Jean up from your place because the parking would be difficult at the wedding reception hall.

Then Jean rings almost as soon as you've arrived at the office on that day. "Hey, we've got a problem. But not to worry, honey, my agile mind has solved it!"

Now you really get worried.

"Baba-san's father died last night. Yueko tells me that we really should drop in and pay our respects, seeing that he's been such a help to us. I lied to her that you had an important business meeting and I would not be able to get in touch with you. So I'm going with Yueko. Look, can you ask Tsuji-san to pick me up from Yueko's place? It's on the way."

You realise that this does not fit in with Jean's white lie but you keep your mouth shut. Tsuji-san walks up to your desk in the open office with that *ringi* paper in his hand but stands off when he sees that you are on the phone.

"Sure, honey. He's right here in front of me now. Consider it fixed."

You put down the phone and ask Tsuji-san, "Do you mind if we take you one street off your route this evening and pick up Jean from a friend's house on the way there? She's got to pay our respects to a good friend whose father died last night."

Tsuji-san's jaw drops and his eyes open wide. It's not like him to show his feelings like that.

Why?

A You are pushing his willingness to drive you to the wedding too far.
B It is inconceivable that Jean should go alone to Baba-san's house, representing both of you.
C It is impossible for Jean to dress suitably for a death visit and a wedding.
D Jean will be smelling of the death house incense.

Comments

A is wrong. But you could have asked Tsuji-san for the added favour in a nicer, more roundabout way.

B will not shock Tsuji-san like that. Baba-san and his family would understand the importance of a major business negotiation. That is, if Jean said it properly.

C is right. But you know you can rely on Jean. Yueko will advise her just what to wear and she'd probably bring a change to Yueko's house.

D is what has shaken Tsuji-san. Not just the incense. It is utterly insensitive of you to go from a funeral or a death visit to a wedding, to bring such terrible bad luck down on Aoi Sudeo and his bride. Not just the smell of incense. "And I thought he was not like the other *gaijin* ..." Tsuji-san would be blaming himself for believing that he had taught you all the ways of the Japanese.

SITUATION 4

The background: You've been through hell with Hirota Takahashi sorting out the details of that tender for ten days. You've seen how the man ticks. He's a down-to-earth guy. No nonsense. And three days ago, after the payments schedule was sorted out, the whole jin-bang went to the *akachochin* and had a real piss-up. Hirota was completely blotto. Just like back home after that hard session with Peter on the Montana deal when you and Peter established a real relationship drinking all night. Well, that's how Jean described it.

Today, you put the tender to bed. So you go out with Hirota and the gang. Everyone sings into the mike. It's a terrific night.

The problem happens when you are walking out of the place. You put your arm around Hirota and tell him, "Hey, Hiro, we're mates, buddy." He freezes. The others in 'the gang' are terribly embarrassed.

Why?

A You've used his first name.
B You are showing a certain amount of indiscipline.
C You put your arm around his shoulders.
D The time to celebrate is not when you've finished the tender but when you've won it.

Comments

A is one reason. Even if Takahashi-san has told you to call him Hirota in his cups, you should not call him Hirota in front of others. And you should not abbreviate his name to Hiro.

B is not likely. The Japanese accept drunken indiscretions and indiscipline fairly liberally, but the fundamentals must never, ever be forgotten. Thus Takahashi-san getting happily sozzled with you at the previous session does not mean that you now have a licence to treat him as your brother.

C is definitely one source of disturbance to the Japanese mind. Body contact should be avoided at all times. Probably the main reason that night.

D is not a culturally biased thing. The Japanese certainly believe in relaxing after a drawn-out series of talks and decisions. Some may have felt that a celebration was premature.

SITUATION 5

Jean rings you. "Sorry to disturb you, Jerry. I know it's my fault. But what with Michelle's bad ear from that crowded swimming pool and Yukiko's refusing to ..."

"Yukiko?"

"The maid, you clot!"

"Ah yes, of course ..."

"With all that, I've completely forgotten about the wedding this evening ..."

"What do yer mean?"

"The present."

"Hell! That's your department."

"Yes, I know, Jerry. There's no need to get all ..."

"So. You want me to get it."

"Yes, darling ..."

"Sheees ..."

You rush into the *depato* and get a lovely set of six wine glasses. They pack it beautifully. Takes a devil of a long time though.

At the reception, you chat with Suzuki-san.

"Got them a lovely set of half a dozen wine glasses," you tell him.

Suzuki-san is suddenly tense. You know he wants to tell you you've made a regular gaffe, but he's Japanese and won't do that.

Why?

A The Japanese don't drink wine.

B You should have given money instead.

C You should have checked the list the couple had left at the *depato*. Suzuki-san has probably also given them half a dozen wine glasses.

D There's something wrong with what you've given them.

Comments

A is true, but the couple could be one of the new cheese and wine set who just love the sophisticated ways of the yuppie westerners.

B is also true. The best thing to do is to follow the traditional system and make it a cash gift.

C is nonsense. You think you are still at home. This sort of uncouth stating what you would like to receive is quite contrary to the Japanese character.

D is your gaffe. Never give six of anything. There is a whole set of do's and don'ts in giving presents, starting from the wrapping. You were right in telling the *depato* that it was a wedding gift so that they would wrap it correctly, but you didn't remember what you read in *Culture Shock Japan*.

SITUATION 6

The background: Tommy Nakajima is not a regular Japanese. He's lived in San Francisco and Santiago and Singapore. The fellow's really been around. His English is perfect. Well, almost.

He's got out of his groove. He can look in from the outside.

The scene: You and the missus and Tommy (actually his name is Tomio, but everyone calls him Tommy) and Michiko (she really enjoyed 'Frisco, she said – real swinger, she is) are lying in the summer sun by your poolside, which costs the company the earth. Then out of the blue you ask, "Tell me about the *Burakumin*."

Tommy turns red.

Why?

A The Japanese cannot take the real hot summer sunshine.
B He took such a big gulp of that pisco-sour. Said he's used to it.
C It's the wrong time to talk about serious things. If you asked Bill that when he's lying unwinding with his Bourbon he'd chew you up and tell you to save it for another day.
D Tommy hates talking of the unpleasant things in Japan.

Comments

D is right. Remember, Tommy is really Nakajima Tomio-san. And you touched on a subject that is anathema.

A is wrong. The skin of the Japanese is not as sensitive to ultra-violet rays as that of some individuals from northern Europe. And the sun in Tokyo is not as strong as it is on the ski slopes in Europe nor in the cloudless-sky countries.

B would be a lively subject of discussion without conclusion at the club. Try it. Ask, "Is it true that the Japanese cannot hold their liquor?" Our bet is that 75% will say 'yes'.

C could be right. But it's got nothing to do with whether he's Japanese or not. It depends on what sort of a bloke Nakajima Tomio-san is.

The *Burakumin* are an absolutely taboo subject. Don't push a guy who appears to be completely westernised.

SITUATION 7

The scene: Monday evening, waiting for dinner in the cramped *apato* where even your bag of golf clubs seems to fill the whole place.

You are reading the English version of the *Nihon Keizai Shimbun*, scowling. "The Japanese government has agreed to the unlimited imports of provided that they are packed in boxes of Japanese pine."

You jolly well know that it would whack up the price at least 30% if it was packed …

"Honey! Did you hear what I said?"

"Uh-uh …"

"Remember how upset you got when we were in India? Well, we don't have to behave like the British raj here."

"Ummmm …"

"Well, what do you think?"

"Mmmmmm …"

"Shall I ask her to eat with us?"

"Her?"

"I don't think you heard me. The maid, Yukiko. Eat with us. Treat her like a human being."

"No. Definitely, no."
Jean's mad with you now. Why?

A Jean does not understand that in Japan one has to keep the servants in their place.
B Jean does not see that Yukiko will be too shy to eat at the table with the family. What with Dickie's endless school stories and the way Shirley snivels at the table when her nose is blocked.
C Yukiko, with her exceptionally good English, is enough of a bad influence on the children. Jean cannot see that.
D Yukiko hates western food.

Comments

A is utter balderdash. The master of the house is obviously not used to servants, like so many expatriates, and should face the fact and sort out how he should treat the housemaid. It's not unlike managing your staff at the factory.

B is right. The Japanese maid will be most uncomfortable eating with the family.

C depends on the maid. Through her, the children could learn a lot about Japan. It's true they may pick up superstitions and other such things from the maid, but one could correct that. It would be most unusual to have a maid who speaks English fluently, but if you did find one, she could have a wonderful, beneficial influence on the children.

D together with *B* are good reasons for rejecting Jean's suggestion. It would be something totally alien to Yukiko-san. It will embarrass her no end. Family dinners would turn into painful nightly routines not only for Yukiko-san but for everyone.

The real reason Jean would be annoyed is because you now think you're the lord and master of the house, since you came to male-chauvinist Japan, and have not explained to her why you said 'no' so quickly and decisively.

SITUATION 8

Tsuji-san has asked you and Jean out to dinner with Naito-san and their wives. You know it's a very special effort on their part to play up to the *gaijin*'s ways of inviting wives. By now both you and Jean have a good relationship with Tsuji-san, though Jean will never get the pronunciation of his name right.

Amid laughter and Tsuji-san saying that he would insist on western democracy that night, and you interrupting to say it wasn't western democracy but Japanese consensus that Tsuji-san was seeking, the order is discussed and Jean suggests *sushi* to finish off with. There is a silence. Tsuji-san and Naito-san (Jean cannot pronounce that name right, either) exchange a knowing look.

Why?

A Jean should never have suggested *sushi*.

B Jean said Naito-san's name wrongly again. It's O.K. with Tsuji-san. He's got to know you. But Naito-san?

C Although Tsuji-san had suggested it would be a consensus order, he hadn't the slightest intention of allowing anyone else to interfere. You suddenly remember that Naito-san didn't make any suggestion.

D Jean should have stayed out of it.

Comments

A is one possible reason. *Sushi* is a snack-like thing. To ask for *sushi* at a grand dinner is like asking for a hamburger for the last course.

B would not upset Naito-san. He's probably heard many uncultured *gaijin* forget to enunciate the *i*.

C is not right, as this is probably not a matter of cultural difference. Just Tsuji-san being the bossy man he is.

D is another possible reason. Jean should have stayed out of it under most circumstances. But Tsuji-san had opened the door to *gaijin* and females to make suggestions. Maybe for his amusement. Maybe he felt he should humour the both of you.

SITUATION 9

You are with the boys after work, again in that dingy *akachochin*. There is much laughter accompanied by much drinking.

You're really relaxed after the fifth. You think you're back home where the guys would ask you to tell them the latest you've heard. You used to know them all. So you tell them the one about the Irish who sent ten thousand men to the Gulf during the Iraqi-Kuwait war in 1991 and now the Mexicans don't know what to do with them.

No one laughs.

Why?

A It's an ethnic joke. Well, in a way …
B The Japanese have no sense of humour whatsoever.
C You shouldn't try to lead in such gatherings. You forgot that you're just a ruddy *gaijin*.
D They immediately thought you were making fun of them.

Comments

D is wrong. They're not *so* sensitive.

A is similarly wrong. They can take ethnic jokes. As long as the jokes against the Japanese come from them. Don't forget that. You can tell that same joke in Dublin if you said the Japanese sent the ten thousand to the Gulf. You probably would have had their laugh if you said it was the Koreans.

There is some truth in *C*. Never forget that you're a *gaijin*. Unless you speak their language absolutely fluently with all the right honorifics and the correct self-effacing phrases. And even then, you may still be regarded as a *gaijin*. Unless you marry one of them. Even then. Or you become a Japanese citizen. If you can, that is. But even then … We could go on and on.

B is such a subjective thing. Humour is to a large extent culturally biased.

Probably the big mistake not listed above is that you started a joke-trading session.

You may be forced to feign laughter, over and over again. The Japanese sense of humour is not exactly the same as the American. Just as the British and French have a different sense of humour.

Take the Japanese one about the boy who asked his illiterate father how to write 'Beware of Fire'. The father told his son to go off to bed and he would have the words for him in the morning, to save face.

The next morning there was a sign from a shop on the dining table.

The boy asked his father, "Why have you put up that sign that says, 'Liquidation sale'?" Ha, ha, ha.

Or they may tell you the one about the two farmers who had their little plots on either side of a small temple. One day some celebrity went there and prayed for some impossible thing and out of the blue it came to him. The temple became famous and a place of pilgrimage overnight.

The farmer on the eastern side of the tumbled-down temple put up a notice and let out his toilet for 100 yen a shot. There were long queues of strained-faced customers. He made a little fortune.

The following year, the farmer on the western side did the same thing. At the end of the day his wife went fiercely at him, "Where the hell were you all day when I was collecting the money without a moment of rest? The money was just pouring in."

"It's been a hard day for me too. I spent the whole day in the other fellow's toilet."

SITUATION 10

Henri L'Abbe has been living and working in Japan for goodness-knows how many years. That's why you decided to use him as a consultant.

"People like him have a wealth of experience that we can tap into and we can save ourselves months, possibly years, of learning time," you said to the president on the overseas call that day. He agreed.

It had been a good afternoon at the prospective buyer's place. Then you and Henri had a few drinks with the *shachoh* (company president) at a tiny little *sushi*-bar around the corner. They seemed to know the fellow very well.

The conversation was mainly on Japanese customs, religion, and table manners. The *shachoh* initially seemed pleased with your interest, but after the third *tokkuri* of *sake* you saw Henri getting edgy and then noticed that the *shachoh* was losing his enthusiasm in answering your endless questions. At about seven he mumbled an excuse and the party broke up.

Henri was glum as you walked to the *chikatetsu* (subway). You knew you had done something wrong.

You asked Henri and he answered gruffly, "It's all those 'whys' of yours."

Why?

A You shouldn't have asked him so much about Shintoism.

B You embarrassed the *shachoh* because he did not know the origin of so many of their customs.

C You don't ask a senior man to teach you table manners.

D You kept asking for logical reasons. You kept asking 'why'.

Comments

A is unlikely. Some Japanese may not like one probing into their religion, like some Jews or Catholics, but there is no general objection to anyone asking questions about Shintoism. However, just to be on the safe side, try to avoid the subject.

B is also not likely. Unless it was a subject that the *shachoh* thought he was an expert on.

Not *C*. The *shachoh* would have been pleased to teach a *gaijin* how to behave himself at table.

It was *D*. You don't keep asking why in Japan.

Henri gave you his belly-full.

"The Japanese don't keep asking why. Sure, they want to know why chemical reactions and mechanical things work, but on matters handed down to them from grandfather to father and father to son, there's no earthly point asking why as far as they are concerned. It's just like that. There are customs and patterns of behaviour that no one would question. No one can change. It was always like that and will be always like that. For ever and ever Amen!"

THE AUTHOR

Rex Shelley, a Eurasian, was born in Singapore in 1930. He was brought up in Malaysia and Singapore and finished his education at the University of Cambridge, England.

He first learnt Japanese during the war, forgot most of it, and then renewed his study of the language with frenzied interest in 1971. He has written an illustrated reference book on Japan, *Cultures of the World: Japan*, and a book on Japanese business style in conjunction with Mitsubishi Corporation, *Words Mean Business*. He has translated many Japanese short stories, a full-length novel, traditional folk tales and modern Japanese poetry. His first novel, *The Shrimp People*, was awarded the top prize by the National Book Development Council of Singapore in 1992. *People of the Pear Tree*, his second novel, and *Culture Shock Japan* received NBDCS book awards in 1994. In 1996, *Island in the Centre*, another novel, was highly commended by the NBDCS.

Mr Shelley runs his own trading company and keeps in touch with Japan through his business and his frequent visits to the country. He is currently serving on the Public Service Commission in Singapore, and has been awarded the Public Service Star twice by the President of the Republic of Singapore. In addition to work, writing, and public service, he paints on fabrics and plays the piano and piano accordion.

INDEX